PRAYER:
THE GREAT CONVERSATION

Prayer:

The Great Conversation

*Straight Answers to Tough
Questions about Prayer*

by

Peter Kreeft

IGNATIUS PRESS   SAN FRANCISCO

Originally published by
Servant Publications
Ann Arbor, Michigan

Cover by Kelly Connelly

Published 1991, Ignatius Press, San Francisco
© 1985 Peter Kreeft
All rights reserved
ISBN 0–89870–357–3
Library of Congress catalogue card number 91–75444
Printed in the United States of America

Contents

for Tom DiLorenzo, Gregory Elmer,
and Ronda Chervin

Preface

THIS BOOK CAN BE USED by itself or as part of a catechism, of which *Yes or No?* was the first volume. *Yes or No?* explored apologetics, reasons for the Christian faith: the objective half. This book explores prayer and the spiritual life: the subjective half. Future volumes will deal with morality and Church.

This catechism is unique for (1) its dialogue form, (2) its ecumenical, "mere Christianity" content, and (3) its orthodox, traditional point of view. Most catechisms are (1) monologue, and therefore sound "preachy," (2) either for Protestants only or for Catholics only, and (3) more often than not written from the point of view of some form of "Christianity-and-water", as C. S. Lewis calls the various current attempts to water down the "full Gospel", the "strong meat" the Church has believed from the beginning.

The dialogue form seems to fit the subject matter, for prayer itself is a dialogue, a "great conversation" with God. In *Yes or No?* the dialogue partners were a believer (Chris the Christian) and an unbeliever (Sal the Seeker). Now Sal has become a new Christian, and Chris pastors Sal in the area of prayer. (Note that "Sal" can stand for "Sally" or "Salvatore", and "Chris" for "Christopher" or "Christine".)

The ecumenical content is not a thin "lowest common denominator", but "the beef", essential Christianity. What Protestants and Catholics agree about is incomparably more important than what they disagree about.

The fact that the point of view is traditional does not mean it is dead or boring—unless C. S. Lewis, G. K. Chesterton, Thomas Merton, John Wesley, Kierkegaard, Newman, Pascal, Luther, Aquinas, Augustine, Paul, and Jesus himself are dead and boring.

Yes or No? was dramatic. It sought the truth with a passion. This book has an even greater drama and passion: not just for the truth about God but for God himself. Prayer is the most exciting experience in human life when it is done correctly, for prayer means touching God.

Dialogue One

Praying Isn't "Saying Your Prayers"

Chris: Well, here we are again in another book!

Sal: The last one worked out all right. Maybe this one will too. What's this one about?

Chris: About the *practice* of the religion you've come to believe in. Your next step.

Sal: Practice? You mean ethics? Morals?

Chris: No, that part will come in another book.

Sal: Going to church, then? Public worship?

Chris: No, though that's part of it too—still another book.

Sal: But I thought those three were the three parts of religion: what you believe, how you live, and what you do in church: words, works, and worship; creed, code, and cult.

Three parts of religion

Chris: That's pretty good. But they're the shell, not the nut; the car, not the engine; the bread, not the meat.

Sal: Well, what's the meat? "Where's the beef?"

Chris: A pretty important question, wouldn't you say?

Sal: And your pretty important answer is—?

11

The essence of Christianity **Chris:** The essence of Christianity is a lived relationship with God, a love affair with God. It's more like marriage than anything else I can think of: a whole shared life. Those other three things we mentioned —shared ideas, shared values, and shared activities— they're only aspects of that shared life.

Sal: Let me get this straight. We talked about theology and doctrine last time, right? What you believe and why you believe it.

Chris: Right.

Sal: And now you're telling me that this isn't the heart of it all?

Chris: Right. Theology is knowing truth *about* God. That's important, all right, but not as important as *knowing* God; just as knowing things about your friend is not as important as knowing your friend.

Sal: I see. Christianity isn't just an idea; it's a relationship.

Chris: Exactly.

Sal: Then where do the ideas come in? The doctrines I've learned to believe—how do they relate to this relationship?

Chris: They're the shape of it, the skeleton. But a skeleton without living flesh is pretty ugly—and dead.

Sal: I see. But flesh without a skeleton can't live either.

Chris: Right you are! Christianity is both. We talked about the intellectual skeleton in our last set of conversations; now we're here to talk about the flesh, the experience of touching God.

Sal: That sounds exciting. I suppose you have a dull name for it?

Chris: Yes, as a matter of fact. Sometimes it's called prayer, sometimes spirituality, sometimes the inner life.

Is prayer exciting? **Sal:** The *word* "prayer" doesn't sound exciting; but the experience of meeting God—really experiencing him, not just having concepts about him—that sure sounds exciting.

Chris: It's the most exciting thing in the world, though in a deep and peaceful sort of way. No one who has ever experienced God in prayer has ever found anything more joyful, not even owning half the world.

Sal: Don't you think most people would laugh at that claim?

Chris: Only the ones who haven't tried both, and they're in no position to compare them then. Experience is the surest teacher.

Sal: But haven't most people tried it? Doesn't almost everyone pray sometimes? Yet they don't seem to get much of a kick out of it.

Chris: Most people dabble in it. They "say a few prayers". But that's like getting only your toes wet in the ocean and then thinking you know what an ocean swim is. Real prayer is like jumping in over your head and letting the waves break over you, even letting the undertow carry you out to sea.

Sal: Sounds scary.

Chris: That's why people avoid it. It *sounds* scary, but it isn't, because the ocean is God, and God is love.

God is love.

Sal: Love can seem scary sometimes, you know.

Chris: You're profoundly right there.

Sal: Love can be like fire.

Chris: Ah, but God's love is the opposite of fire in one way: the closer you get to it, the less you're burned. It seems painful and scary only at the outer edges.

Sal: Also, fire doesn't care about you.

Chris: Right again. And God does. In fact, right this minute he's longing to have you come closer to him.

Sal: You mean literally?

Chris: Yes.

Sal: But I thought God was eternal and perfect and had no needs.

Chris: Yes, but he's a person, not just a force. He has a will, a heart, a desire. He's *love*, Sal! And love is longing, yearning. What meaning could we possibly give to "God is love" if that love were cold and correct and uncaring and calculating? Love always cares. And since God is infinite love, his caring and desiring and yearning are infinite.

Sal: Wow! It's hard to square that with my picture of God being eternal.

Chris: Yes, it is. But don't let either truth go, just because you can't understand how they fit together.

Sal: What does God yearn for, then?

Chris: The one thing he can't do himself, the one thing he can't give to himself and only you can give him.

Sal: Is there such a thing?

Chris: Yes.

Sal: What is it, then?

Chris: Your free love, your free choice to come closer to him, your "yes" to his offer of intimacy. What we just talked about.

God wants you to pray. *Sal:* You mean God wants me to learn how to pray?

Chris: Yes.

Sal: You mean right now, this very moment, God is waiting for me?

Chris: Yes! God wants us to have these conversations. God wants people to read this book and practice it. That's why its author wrote it.

Sal: What do you mean?

Chris: For God. Not only to help people satisfy their desire for God, but also to help God satisfy his desire for them. To make God happy.

Sal: We can make God happy?

Chris: Sure.

Sal: How can that be?

Chris: Because he really loves us, really cares. He's our Father. We're his babies. A baby's parents really care that the baby learns to walk and talk.

Sal: So prayer is talking to God, right?

Chris: And walking with God.

Sal: Well, I want to learn that art.

Chris: It is an art. And anyone can learn it.

Sal: Can you teach me?

Chris: Only a little. For advanced lessons, you'll have to go to wiser and holier Christians than I. But if you want some beginner's lessons, O.K. That's all a beginner like me can teach. You can't give what you don't have (though preachers and teachers often try).

Sal: It's a deal, then. Where do we start?

Chris: Well, before we go any further in talking about how to pray, we'd better define our terms, don't you think?   *Defining prayer*

Sal: Sure. So define "prayer" for me, please.

Chris: No, *you* will if you want to learn. What do you think it is?

Sal: Something you say to God, I guess.

Chris: Do you *say* prayers, or do you *pray*?

Sal: What's the difference?

Chris: All the difference in the world. Like the difference between "blowing a kiss" to someone and kissing them.

Sal: Prayer is like kissing God?

Chris: Yes, and wrestling with God, and just sitting with God . . .

Sal: I thought it was *mental* communication.

Chris: More than that. The essence of real communication is always a real touching, even among us.

Sal: Physically?

Chris: No, spiritually. A touching of spirits. Surface communication is just an exchange of words. Real communication is an exchange of persons.

Sal: Why isn't real communication exchanging words?

Chris: Because computers or tape decks can do that.

Sal: O.K., but prayer *is* talking to God, right? Isn't that words?

Chris: And walking with God, remember?

Sal: O.K., but the talking part? . . .

Chris: Is talking *with* God, not just *to* God. You have to *be* with somebody before you can talk with them. Computers can talk *to* you, but not *with* you because they can't *be* with you. There's nobody there. No presence, no person.

Sal: I see.

Chris: And here's another reason prayer is talking *with* God, not just *to* God: half of it is listening, or should be. Maybe much more than half.

Sal: So we don't have to say much? Good prayers are short?

Chris: Yes. The best prayer of all, the one Jesus taught us to pray, is very short. All the prayers Jesus prayed in the Gospels are short. Yet he spent a lot of time in prayer. He was constantly going off into the desert to pray, sometimes all night. So if he spent a lot of time and only did a little talking, he must have done a lot of listening, right?

Sal: Right.

Chris: And what better model, what better teacher to teach us how to pray, could there ever be, than Jesus himself?

Sal: You've convinced me. So how do I listen to God in prayer?

Chris: That's such an important question that I think we should take a whole conversation for it later, O.K.?

Sal: O.K. And how about talking about the "walking with God" part too? Can I pray as I live and work—all the time?

Chris: Yes, you can. And we'll talk about that in another conversation too.

Sal: Can you just tell me what it means now, basically?

Chris: Sure. The Bible describes it as something Adam and Eve did in the Garden of Eden: God "walked with them in the cool of the evening". It often describes a holy person, like Enoch, as one who "walked with God". It means knowing God.

Walking with God

Sal: Not theology.

Chris: No, friendship.

Sal: So theology isn't really worth all that much then, right?

Chris: Wrong! Don't put down theology. One thing isn't made worthless by another thing being even more valuable. A billionaire doesn't make a millionaire a pauper.

Sal: But theology's just a road map. Prayer is traveling. Right?

Chris: Right. But did you ever try to travel in unknown places without a road map?

Prayer and theology

Sal: I see your point. But didn't you say that creed, code, and cult were only like an outer shell of a nut?

Chris: Yes.

Sal: And prayer gets you inside?

Chris: Yes.

Sal: And the point is to touch the nut, to actually eat it.

Chris: Yes.

Sal: But to do that, you have to break the shell first.

Chris: Yes, but not in a destructive way. The shell is essential; it protects the nut inside.

Sal: And the nut is prayer?

Chris: The nut is God himself, experienced in praying.

Sal: I see. Tell me, why do you keep saying "praying" and not just "prayer"?

Chris: Because "pray" is an active verb. Praying is something you *do*; it makes Christianity more like a laboratory than a classroom.

Keeping a prayer journal

Sal: Wouldn't it be a good idea to keep a laboratory journal?

Chris: Sometimes, yes. But keep it short and simple and focused on God, not yourself. Don't get ingrown eyeballs.

Sal: Would keeping a journal tend to do that, do you think?

Chris: With some people, yes; with others, no.

Sal: Well, I like the idea of keeping a personal journal. Like a private diary. Something only I can do. My unique signature on it. A present to offer to God when it's finished.

Chris: It may get finished, but *you* never will, not in this life.

Sal: I have one more question for you today, Chris. Most Christians pray, right?

Chris: Right.

Sal: Then why are there so few who have the kind of friendship with God, this intimacy, that we're talking about?

Chris: Why do you think it's so few?

Sal: You know what I mean.

Chris: No, I don't. You have to say it.

Sal: Well, even preachers—even good and sincere ones—seem to be mouthing words most of the time. When you meet one who really seems to know God personally, you recognize him. He stands out. You know what I mean, don't you?

Chris: Yes.

Sal: Well, why are there so few?

Chris: How do you know there are only a few? Can you look into people's hearts?

Sal: No . . .

Chris: So maybe that dull and utterly ordinary person is really doing the most exciting thing in human life: walking with God. Maybe that old bum is one of God's very closest friends.

Sal: I see. I was judging, and judging by appearances. I guess I'd better stop looking at them and start looking at myself. Because that's the one person I *do* know from the inside and the one person I can do something about.

Chris: Boy, you learn really fast, Sal!

Sal: I don't want to keep God waiting. Well, let's begin, instead of *talking* about beginning!

Can you tell who God's friends are?

Dialogue Two

Why We Can't Find Time to Pray

Chris: Sal, I think we should begin at the beginning, don't you?

Sal: Of course.

Chris: Even if the beginning is the very hardest place to begin?

The first step is the hardest.

Sal: What in the world do you mean by that?

Chris: I mean that the very first step in praying is the hardest step of all.

Sal: What is it?

Chris: Before I answer that question, I want to know whether you really want to *begin* there, with the hardest thing? Or do you just want to *know* what it is, to satisfy your curiosity?

Sal: Why do you answer my question with a question?

Chris: Because just answering your question, "What's the beginning?" isn't enough. You have to *do* it, not just know it. So I want to know whether it's just your mind or also your will that's asking that question. Are you ready to do it?

Sal: Of course I am.

Chris: No, not "of course".

Sal: Well, I am. Why do you think I'm here with you? To learn to *do* praying, not just learn *about* it.

Taking time to pray

Chris: All right, then, here's the first thing, the hardest thing, and the most essential thing of all. It's simply taking time to pray.

Sal: That sounds pretty simple.

Chris: Simple, yes. Easy, no.

Sal: Why do you say it's the most essential thing of all? And how do you do it?

Chris: It's the most essential thing of all just because it's not a matter of *how* you do it at all, but of *whether* you do it. Like being born, or cooking: *how* you do it is less important than *whether* you do it. You can find thousands of books on prayer that give you methods of praying, hundreds of "hows"; but they do you no good at all unless you actually pray. Otherwise, it's like just reading a cookbook instead of cooking. You can't eat a cookbook!

Sal: That's obvious. I know all that. Why do you have to make that obvious point?

Chris: Because once you start praying, you'll probably find hundreds of surprisingly good excuses to stop, hundreds of good reasons to postpone it to some other time, hundreds of Martha things to choke out the one Mary thing, the "one thing necessary".

Martha and Mary: Luke 10:38–42

Sal: What do you mean, "Martha things" and "Mary thing"?

Chris: Don't you know the story of Mary and Martha in the Gospel?

Sal: I think so. Where is it?

Chris: Right here . . . let's see, Luke 10, I think.

Sal: You carry a Bible with you?

Chris: A little New Testament plus Psalms. Fits in the back pocket nicely.

Sal: What for?

Chris: Does a cowboy carry his pistol?

Sal: O.K., get out your pistol and shoot. Let's read the passage.

Chris: Here it is. "As Jesus and his disciples went on their way, he came to a village where a woman named Martha welcomed him in her home. She had a sister named Mary, who sat down at the feet of the Lord and listened to his teaching. Martha was upset over all the work she had to do, so she came and said, 'Lord, don't you care that my sister has left me to do all the work by myself? Tell her to come and help me!' The Lord answered her, 'Martha, Martha! You are worried and troubled over so many things, but just one thing is needed. Mary has chosen the right thing, and it will not be taken away from her.' "

Sal: And what was that one thing?

Chris: A footnote to that verse refers to Psalm 27:4. Let's look that up, so we can answer your question with God's words, not just mine. Here it is: "One thing I have desired of the Lord, that will I seek: that I may dwell in the house of the Lord all the days of my life, to behold the beauty of the Lord and to inquire in his temple."

Sal: His temple? In church?

Chris: In prayer. In his presence. What Mary sought —and found. Martha put prayer second to work, and Jesus said Mary's order of priorities was the right one, not Martha's.

Sal: But Martha was doing good work. She was probably setting the table for Mary and Jesus. Why did Jesus put her down for that?

Chris: Not for that; for worrying, and for hopping on one foot.

Sal: Hopping on one foot?

Chris: We're meant to walk on two feet: prayer and work. Martha was all work and no prayer.

Prayer and work

Sal: I see. Two feet work better than one.

Chris: Much more than twice as well. One plus one is more than two here.

Sal: But isn't there a danger of neglecting work too?

Chris: For prayer? In our society? Tell me, who do you know who prays so much he has no time for work?

Sal: Nobody.

Chris: Right. But how many say they have no time for prayer because of work?

Sal: Just about everybody.

Chris: Then that passage in the Gospels is really relevant, really needed in our society, right?

Sal: Right. But all Mary did was sit at Jesus' feet and listen. Is that what prayer is?

Chris: Yes! That's the essence, anyway.

Sal: But that's easy!

Chris: No, it isn't. To stop the Martha mind, the hurrying and worrying mind—just to stop and to give God some time—that's hard.

Sal: Why is it so hard?

Chris: Do you admit that it is?

Sal: I guess so. The little I've tried seems to teach me that.

Chris: The more you try, the more you'll learn that.

The problem doesn't go away. *Sal:* But I don't understand why. This is a real problem for me, Chris. Let's be totally honest, O.K.? I'm a pretty new Christian, a beginner, and I thought I had this problem only because I was so new. But now I hear you saying the problem's not going to go away. You must know that by experience, so you must have it too.

Chris: I sure do.

Sal: Well, then, maybe you can help me. That's one thing I just don't understand about myself. It's just totally irrational.

Chris: What's that?

Sal: Every time I pray, it helps tremendously, both inside and outside. I feel a real joy, either then or afterward, and a peace, and things seem to fall into place.

Chris: Wonderful. What's the problem?

Sal: I just don't *do* it. I don't pray much. I give excuses, like Martha. But I know better. Why do I run away from the thing that gives me such joy and peace? Why doesn't prayer seem joyful to me *before* I do it, even though it seems joyful *when* I do it and *after* I do it? I seem to fear it. At least I run away from it. I find hundreds of excuses. I give up five minutes of joy for five hours of trivia. Why? It's like an addiction —it's irrational. And yet it's not any one thing I'm addicted to—it's not that I love something else so much. It's that I run away from doing what Mary did, just stopping the motion and sitting at Jesus' feet and listening. Why is that so hard?

Why run away from prayer?

Chris: Sal, I know what you're saying. Believe me, that's my problem too. I wondered about that for a long time before I found the answer. It's so simple that once you see it, it's obvious. You ask yourself how you could have missed it. Yet I missed it for years.

Sal: Well, don't keep me in suspense! Why do I run from prayer?

Chris: Think for a minute. What is there in you that wants God's presence, God's face, God's light?

Sal: The deepest desire of my heart, I think.

Chris: I believe you, Sal. And remember, whatever we really seek, we really find. Remember that promise?

Sal: Yes. Thanks for reminding me. But . . .

Chris: Yes, "but". What else is there? What is there in you that doesn't want to stand face to face with God? It's not work; that's just the excuse you give. What in you fears the light? What plant grows only in the darkness? What would be killed by God's light?

Sal: I don't know. Do you?

Chris: Yes.

Sal: Then you're wiser than I am.

Chris: No. I didn't figure it out for myself. I found it in God's Word.

Sal: Well, what is it?

Sin   *Chris:* Sin.

Sal: Oh.

Chris: Sin is real, you know. It's like cancer. It's *in* us. It's not just something we *do* now and then; it's something we *are*. Saint Paul called it "the old man", or the Adam in us, "the flesh"—fallen human nature. *That* fears God and whispers in the ear of your unconscious mind, "Be careful! Don't get too close to God. He's a killer, you know." And the voice speaks the truth. God *does* want to kill that cancer in you.

Sal: This sounds spooky. I don't have another person in me, do I? How can it speak with a voice like that? How can it *know* anything?

Chris: Look at it in this way: the mind and will of the God you serve is *in* you in a sense, isn't it? Isn't he?

Sal: Yes.

Chris: And do you serve him with *all* your heart and soul and mind and strength? Do you obey "the first and greatest commandment" perfectly?

Sal: No.

Chris: Then you partly serve another.

Sal: Who?

Chris: You might not believe me if I told you. But would you believe Jesus?

Sal: Yes. What does he say?

The Devil hates *Chris:* It's the Devil. He wants your soul. He's terri-
prayer. fied of God, as darkness is terrified of light. He's the

source of the cancer of sin, though we're to blame for listening to him. He doesn't dare let you pray, because when you stand face to face with God like that, God's light destroys the Devil's colonies of darkness in you.

Sal: Oh!

Chris: And *that's* why you give excuses for running away from prayer.

Sal: That's terrible!

Chris: Yes, it is. And now that you know where this impulse to give excuses comes from, you also know what to do about it.

Sal: I sure do. But it's still just knowledge. I have to translate it into action.

Chris: Exactly.

Sal: Chris, I really want to pray, and I don't want to give a hundred silly excuses, but there's one excuse that almost always seems to be true. . . .

Chris: Don't tell me, let me guess.

Sal: Go ahead.

Chris: You don't have enough time. You're too busy. Something else always seems to come up.

Too busy to pray?

Sal: How did you know?

Chris: From experience.

Sal: Yours too?

Chris: Mine and just about everyone else I know.

Sal: Then it's true.

Chris: No. It's an excuse.

Sal: So?

Chris: Whenever you start giving excuses for anything, that's the time to start doing the thing you're giving excuses for not doing.

Sal: But I'm not a minister or priest or nun. I'm just . . .

Chris: Just a Christian.

Sal: I'm a practical person.

Chris: Prayer is the most practical thing you can do.

Sal: How can taking time away from something that just *has* to be done be practical?

Chris: Do you remember the story of Jesus multiplying the little boy's five loaves and two fishes and feeding five thousand people from it?

Sal: Sure, but what does that have to do with it?

Chris: He does the same thing with time as he does with loaves and fishes. In fact, he does it with everything you freely give to him. He multiplies it and gives it back to you.

God can multiply time.

Sal: Time too, huh?

Chris: Yes.

Sal: How can I be sure of that?

Chris: Only by trying it.

Sal: I'm just so terribly busy lately . . .

Chris: It's *especially* when you're terribly busy that you need to take time to pray, so that God can multiply your time.

Sal: You mean I won't have to sacrifice any time after all?

Chris: Oh, no, the sacrifice is real. I didn't say *that*. You'll have to say "no" to something to say "yes" to God. But God will give you back much, much more than you give to him.

Sal: That sounds awfully mystical. How does he do that?

Chris: He's the author of all time. He gives out time in the first place—usually at a constant rate. But he can change the rate. Haven't you noticed that people who pray, people who are close to God, seem to have more time? Like Mary instead of like Martha.

Sal: Not fussing and worrying. I think I see how it works. Martha *wasted* a lot of time hopping around on one foot, right?

Chris: Right.

Sal: It seems so strange that praying is so practical.

Chris: Not strange at all. It's like charging your batteries for later use. When crises come, big ones or little ones, you're going to pull on your resources, your inner strength, your spiritual batteries. After months of not praying much, you're vulnerable, weak, brittle. It's like not eating right, or not exercising.

Sal: Prayer is soul food, eh?

Chris: Exactly. Believe me, it's practical.

Sal: I believe you, but I still can't seem to find time for it.

Chris: I understand.

Sal: You do? It seems so foolish.

Chris: Not totally. Because it can't be done, you know. You'll never find time to pray.

Sal: What?

Chris: You have to *make* time to pray. It takes sacrifice. Something has to go, usually something that seems important. Remember Mary and Martha. Do you think Mary was selfish and didn't *want* to help her sister with the housework? Do you think the work didn't need to be done? There's always something that needs to be done. You just have to say "no" to it, sacrifice it, for "the one thing necessary". *You have to make time.*

Sal: I see. It takes effort to start, then.

Chris: It sure does. It takes a deliberate, conscious effort of will. And there's no gimmick for that, no method, no "how". The first step is just deciding to *do* it. Not just *wishing*, but *deciding*, willing. If you really decide to do it, you'll do it. If you don't end up doing it, that means you didn't really decide to do it.

Sal: I see. It's so simple, it's hard.

Chris: Because there's no way, no method, no means to that end, no prior step. It *is* the prior step, the first step. But it's also easy for the same reason. Nothing else has to be done first. You just do it.

Sal: O.K., I'm going to do it, come hell or high water.

Chris: Great.

Sal: But there are still other questions to be answered, like where and when and how.

Chris: Right. But now these questions are no longer excuses to avoid praying, but ways of carrying out your decision to pray. And that is the most important thing of all, the most important thing in this whole book.

Sal: O.K., I've settled that. What about the where and when and how now? Do you have any advice for me there?

Where to pray   *Chris:* Yes, and it comes from experience—not just mine but that of millions of Christians down through the centuries. First, as to *where* you pray, the Church has solved half of that problem for you by setting aside special places for public worship every Sunday: the Church has invented churches, following the lead of the Jewish temple. But we have to invent our own private churches too, for private prayer.

Sal: Won't any place do?

Chris: It should be a definite place.

Sal: Why?

Chris: Because "praying anywhere" can easily become "praying nowhere", just as "praying anytime" can easily become "praying at no time". Everything in general becomes nothing in particular.

Sal: O.K., *what* place, then?

Chris: Some special place where you can be alone without being bothered and interrupted and distracted. Maybe your bedroom, or your desk, or even the bathroom, if you can't get alone any other place.

Sal: How about outdoors?

Chris: Fine, if it's accessible, like a backyard or a porch, or the woods if you happen to live nearby. Just as long as it's some special place you keep coming back to every day. That makes it a sacred place, a holy place. There aren't many sacred places left in today's secularized world, so the mere fact of your making one is a great achievement.

Sal: O.K., what about *when*?

Chris: Again, any time will do, but it should be a definite, regular time, the same time each day.

When to pray

Sal: For the same reason, right? Sacred time, like sacred space?

Chris: Yes. And because "anytime" becomes "no time".

Sal: What time do most people find works best?

Chris: A time when they're not going to be disturbed. For many people, the only two times like that are late at night or early in the morning, just after getting up or just before going to bed.

Sal: Most people say their prayers before bedtime, don't they?

Chris: Yes, and that's O.K. for "saying your prayers" but not so good for *praying*, because you're usually too tired. God deserves prime time, not junk time, leftovers. And you do too.

Sal: What do you mean, I do too?

Chris: God wants you to pray for your sake, not his. He doesn't need your prayers; you do.

Sal: Oh.

Chris: But even if you pray early in the morning—the best time for most people—you should take at least a few minutes at night too.

Praying at night

Sal: To say goodbye as well as hello.

Chris: Yes. To review the day and thank God for all of it and commit it to his hands. And because sleep is a little like death.

Sal: I see. And how much time should I take in the morning?

Chris: I think there's no one answer to that question that's right for everybody, but I'd suggest at least fifteen minutes to begin with.

Sal: Fifteen minutes?

Chris: Yes. Do you think that's too much or too little?

Sal: It doesn't *sound* like too much.

Chris: It may *feel* like too much once you start to do it.

Sal: Why?

Is prayer boring?   *Chris:* Because the Devil is going to try to make you feel bored. He's terrified when you pray, remember? And he's a liar. One of his most successful lies is that prayer is boring.

Sal: That's a lie?

Chris: Of course.

Sal: You sound awfully certain. It certainly feels boring to me sometimes.

Chris: It may *feel* boring, but it *isn't*. The Devil may manipulate our feelings, but he can't change reality. You look skeptical. Here—I'll prove it to you. What *is* prayer?

Sal: Getting close to God. Sitting at Jesus' feet.

Chris: Right. And is God boring?

Sal: I guess not.

Chris: I know not. He's the origin of all joy and all beauty. He's the least boring thing in all reality.

Sal: O.K., you've proved it all right. Prayer isn't boring. But it still seems boring sometimes. Does it *have* to be fifteen minutes?

Chris: No . . . five minutes *every* day is better than fifteen minutes every other day. But why do you want to cut it down? If you could get close to the person you love the most only once a day, would you try to cut down on that time?

Sal: Of course not.

Chris: Well, you see what follows with regard to God, don't you?

Sal: I think so.

Chris: Let's make sure. What's the first and greatest commandment of God, both for Jews and Christians?

Sal: That's easy. Love God with all your heart and soul.

Chris: Right. And do you want to do that?

Sal: Sure.

Chris: So you want to get closer to him, right? Love always wants to get closer, doesn't it?

Sal: Yes.

Chris: And prayer is getting closer to God, right?

Sal: Right.

Chris: So therefore you want to pray more, not less.

Sal: Therefore I *should* want to.

Chris: It's *all* "should", starting with the first commandment. None of us obey that perfectly. But we want to, don't we?

Sal: Yes.

Chris: So we want to get closer to God, right?

Sal: Yes.

You should want to pray more.

Chris: So we *want* to pray more, right?

Sal: Yes. I want to. But I don't.

Chris: But we said a little while ago that to really want this; to will it, not just to wish it; to deliberately decide to do it, is to do it. Didn't we agree on that?

Sal: Yes.

Chris: Then you *will* pray more, not less, if you really want to.

Sal: I guess so. And if I don't, I don't really want to. So I can't give the excuse "I want to, but . . ."

Chris: Exactly.

Sal: But I can't pray all day!

Chris: We were talking about fifteen minutes, remember? Not all day. And you were trying to cut that to five. (By the way, all the saints say at least an hour.)

Sal: Oops. You got me there.

Chris: *God* wants to get you, not me.

Sal: To yell at me for being such a fool?

Chris: No, to give you a big hug and tell you he loves you. That's why you're such a fool: because you run away from *that* God.

Fifteen minutes with God

Sal: Got me again. But . . . but I don't think I have fifteen minutes of things to say to God every day.

Chris: Then you'd better spend more time listening to him. Because he has more than fifteen minutes of things to say to you.

Sal: In words?

Chris: Most of it's not in words. Most of love's not in words.

Sal: And if he's got more than fifteen minutes of stuff to tell me . . .

Chris: Then you'd better be listening for more than fifteen minutes a day. The whole day, in fact. Listening to other people's needs is listening to God. Noticing simple, natural beauty, hearing music, even confronting the challenge of pain and problems—that can all be listening to God too.

Sal: Then prayer is all day.

Chris: It should be, yes. But that doesn't mean you can give up the special time. That's like the energizing center, the center of the circle.

Sal: Can you really develop the habit of praying all the time?

Chris: Yes. Saint Paul tells us, "pray without ceasing". He wouldn't tell us to do something impossible.

Sal: Is there a way of developing that art?

Chris: Yes. We'll talk about that another day.

Sal: Why do so few people do it then?

Chris: How do you know how many people are doing it? You can't *see* it.

Sal: Oh, right. But people are so busy today. Don't you think people are busier today and pray less?

Chris: Yes, I do.

Sal: Why do you think that's so?

Chris: Why do *you* think?

Sal: I guess because there's just more to do. The world is so complex. There's been so much progress.

Progress and prayer

Chris: More that we *have* to do?

Sal: Yes.

Chris: Then we're less free, aren't we?

Sal: In that way, yes.

Chris: Is that progress?

Sal: No, but . . . are you saying we were better off 300 years ago, before the Industrial Revolution?

Chris: In some ways, yes.

Sal: What ways?

Chris: We didn't have a thousand little things to distract us: things like rockets and skyscrapers.

Sal: *Little* things?

Chris: Spiritually little, yes. But we did have two very big things that helped us to pray better and more, and those two precious things have been almost totally abolished from our lives by so-called "progress".

Sal: What two things?

Chris: Leisure and silence.

Leisure and silence

Sal: But we have a shorter work week than ever. People are going on vacations all the time. We have a lot of leisure.

Chris: Not in our spirits, we don't. Even our vacations are usually high speed, nose-to-the-grindstone things. We're exhausted after they're over. Ask the average person if he has any free time today, any leisure time. What answer do you get?

Sal: Nobody seems to have enough time for anything. But how can that be? Our machines do our work for us so efficiently. . . . How can labor-saving devices abolish leisure?

Chris: They didn't. We did. Martha, remember?

The lie of "progress"   *Sal:* Wow! A whole civilization of Marthas. What a strange kind of progress.

Chris: I don't call it progress.

Sal: What do you call it?

Chris: Another lie from the Devil.

Sal: What lie?

Chris: That something that makes it harder for us to pray, harder for us to listen to God, can be progress. That running from the light is progress.

Sal: But you can't turn back the clock!

Chris: Sure you can! If a clock tells the wrong time, isn't that exactly what you do?

Sal: But progress and history aren't like a clock. You can't turn them back.

Chris: Why not? Didn't we make them, just as we made clocks? And if we made a mistake, shouldn't we correct it?

Sal: We can't dismantle our civilization! We can't throw away all our machines!

Chris: Who said we should? I just want a little silence and a little leisure. Why does that mean dismantling a whole civilization? Why should it be so extreme? That's as silly as what you said a few minutes ago, when I said you should take fifteen minutes a day for prayer, and you objected that you couldn't pray all day.

Sal: It's hard to get even a little prayer in and hard to get even a little of the silence and leisure you need for prayer.

Chris: Yes, it is.

Sal: Some "progress"!

Chris: But there's a good side to even that.

Sal: What?

Chris: Today we have to fight much harder to pray, but fighters become tough and strong. It's hard to find God in the modern world. So to do it, you have to fight for it. It becomes more precious because of that. You don't take it for granted. Once you've resisted the pressures and taken time for prayer, you've overcome a whole world, a whole civilization.

We have to fight to pray.

Sal: I see why you said the first step was the hardest. And also the most important. A whole world stands in the way.

Chris: But "what does it profit a man if he gains the whole world but loses his own soul?"

Sal: Jesus said that, didn't he?

Chris: Yes. Pretty practical, wasn't he?

Dialogue Three

How to Get Free from Your Feelings

Sal: Chris, isn't it strange that the simplest of all our conversations was also the longest?

Chris: The last one, you mean?

Sal: Yes.

Chris: That's because even though it had only one point to make, and a very simple one—just to *do* it, to set aside fifteen minutes of time every day to pray —yet it was the most important point of all: getting started. So we had to deal with the obstacles to it, just because it's so important. Now that we've taken the time we needed to make that simple point, we can go more quickly through the complex points.

Sal: What complex points?

Chris: How to pray. *How to pray*

Sal: Many books have been written about that, haven't they?

Chris: Yes.

Sal: Then how can we deal with it so quickly?

Chris: Well, not *so* quickly. But I think that all I or anyone else can give you here is a little help. I can't tell you how to pray any more than I can tell you how to sing, or how to write.

Sal: Why not?

Chris: For two reasons, I think. For one thing, it's mostly practice, not theory, not words. In the second place, you have to develop your own way. There's no one technique that's best for everyone, just as in singing—opera is best for one singer, country western for another.

Sal: But there are some general principles, aren't there?

Chris: Oh, yes. And there are methods and styles that millions have used profitably, and you probably will too.

Sal: Is there any way that's good for everyone?

One good prayer   *Chris:* I'm not sure, except for one: the one taught by Jesus himself, what we call the "Lord's Prayer", the "Our Father".

Sal: How do you know that's for everyone?

Chris: Why, because Jesus taught it, of course. It was his answer to his disciples' request, "Teach us to pray." And Jesus is the teacher for the whole world.

Sal: Oh.

Chris: You sound sort of disappointed.

Sal: Not in Jesus, certainly. But in your answer to my question how to pray. I thought you'd give me a technique instead of a prayer.

Chris: But when Jesus was asked, "Teach us to pray", he gave us a prayer instead of a technique.

Sal: Yes . . .

Chris: Why is that disappointing to you?

Sal: Because all the other great teachers and spiritual masters and gurus give techniques, don't they?

Chris: So what if they do? Are they the standard you measure Jesus by? Or is he the standard you measure them by?

Sal: So it looks like Jesus doesn't believe much in technique.

Chris: It looks like it. Maybe that's because prayer is like love.

Sal: What do you mean?

Chris: The "How to Do It" manuals just miss the point.

Sal: I see. So you're advising me to make the Lord's Prayer my only way to pray?

Chris: Of course not, not the *only* way. But the *first* way. It's the one prayer you can pray with total confidence that God wants you to pray this way. Many other kinds of prayer may be good too, but you can never be quite as absolutely sure that any prayer you may happen to like is also what God wills for you.

Sal: Oh. I guess that makes a big difference, doesn't it?

What makes the biggest difference?

Chris: All the difference in the world: to know that God's will and not just yours is behind your prayer. It's like the difference between an ocean and a raindrop.

Sal: You mean you can't stop an ocean or God's will?

Chris: Exactly. God's will is always done. So when you know your prayer lines up with his will, you *know* it's going to be answered.

Sal: So when our prayers aren't answered . . .

Chris: It's because they're only *our* prayers. His are always answered. Our will isn't always done; his is.

Sal: But if he always gets his way, why does he ask us to pray? He can do anything without us, can't he?

Chris: Sure he can.

Sal: Then why did he tell us to pray?

Why pray for things?

Chris: To give us the dignity of being real causes.

Sal: What do you mean?

Chris: He could have done all our bodily work for us too. But then we'd be nothing. And a lover doesn't want his beloved to be nothing.

Sal: I see. It's for us, not for him. But we've been talking only about asking for things; what about other kinds of prayer? What about just sitting at his feet and listening? What about wordless meditation? Aren't they things he wills for us too?

Chris: Yes, and we should talk more about them later.

Sal: How do we know for sure that they're his will for us too?

Chris: The same way we know the Lord's Prayer is. He's told us.

Sal: He's told us to pray wordlessly?

Chris: Yes.

Sal: Where?

Chris: In Scripture: "Be still and know that I am God."

Sal: So prayer has to be based on Scripture.

Chris: I'm not saying never to use a method of prayer if you can't find it in Scripture. But if you *can*, that means you can be sure it's what God wants you to do, and then you can pray in perfect confidence.

Sal: Even if the scriptural prayer doesn't seem to do anything for you?

Chris: What do you mean, "do anything for you"?

Sal: Turn you on, give you any feeling of closeness to God.

Feelings are unreliable. *Chris:* You can't use your feelings as your spiritual thermometer, you know.

Sal: Why not?

Chris: They're unreliable and dependent on a thousand things: what you had to eat, and whether you just had a fight with your friend, and even atmospheric pressure.

Sal: But I thought it was necessary to *experience* God, not just to think about him. Don't you have to know him personally?

Chris: Yes! But that experience isn't only feelings, or first of all feelings.

Sal: What is it, then, if it's not concepts and it's not feelings?

Chris: Faith.

Sal: And that's not concepts *or* feelings?

Chris: No. Saint Paul calls it "seeing through a glass, darkly"—through a smudged mirror. Saint John of the Cross calls it "the dark night of the soul". It's like flying in fog: you can't go by sight. You have to go by your instruments.

Sal: How can you put down reason and feeling like that? Didn't God give them to us?

Chris: Yes, and I'm not putting them down. Is it putting down a rose to say you can't take your temperature with it?

Sal: No, but . . . what's the connection?

Chris: Reason and feeling are not the thermometer God gave us for our souls, or the telescope he gave us to know him with. That's faith.

We know God by faith.

Sal: Why can't reason and feeling be guides too?

Chris: Because they keep changing, and faith doesn't.

Sal: Sure it does.

Chris: *Your* faith does; *the* faith doesn't.

Sal: What do you mean by that distinction?

Chris: That *your* faith comes from inside you, just like your reason and your feelings, but *the* faith comes from God. The faith is simply the truth, objective truth.

Sal: How can you claim that?

Chris: Because it's what God revealed, what God told us, God's Word. That's why it's simply truth. Jesus said, "Thy word is truth." You believe that, don't you?

We had a whole long series of conversations about it, remember?

Sal: Yes, I remember. It's just that it takes time getting used to this new way of thinking. Almost everybody in the world seems to think faith is only subjective, something you conjure up inside yourself.

Chris: You see that that's a terrible mistake, don't you?

Sal: Yes. But *our* faith, inside us, is precious too.

The object of faith is fact. *Chris:* Certainly! But it has an object, and its object is *the* faith, which is fact. The object of faith is fact, not feeling.

Sal: Fact?

Chris: Yes. The facts God revealed to us. There's a saying about faith, fact, and feeling: There are these three people walking along a wall. The first is Fact, the second is Faith, and the third is Feeling. As long as Faith keeps his eyes on Fact, he stays on the wall, and Feeling comes along too. But when Faith takes his eyes off Fact in front of him and turns around to see how Feeling is doing, both Faith and Feeling fall off the wall.

Sal: I think I see.

Chris: Fact is like a locomotive, you see, and feeling is like a caboose. It's not the caboose that pulls the train.

Sal: These facts—you mean everything in Scripture?

Chris: Yes, but of course some things are more important than others.

Sal: What facts are especially important for prayer?

The Creed *Chris:* The main facts of the Creed, of course: that God created the universe and us, for one thing. So we pray not to some creature in the universe, but the perfect and all-powerful Creator of it all. That God became one of us to save us from sin, for another thing. That shows his love, of course, the character of the God we pray to. Even events like the temple curtain splitting in half when Jesus died . . .

Sal: What does *that* have to do with prayer?

Chris: The curtain separated the Holy of Holies from the outer part of the temple. When it was torn miraculously in half at the moment Christ died, that showed us that we now have access to the Holy of Holies, to God's own dwelling, because of what Jesus did.

Sal: How did that work?

Chris: I don't know exactly *how* it worked. But it happened. That's a fact, and our faith is founded on facts. The point is the relation between facts and feelings. If you believe the facts, you can forget about the feelings; they'll come, they'll take care of themselves.

Sal: I get it. If you believe God really hears you and really cares, then you'll naturally feel more confident.

Chris: Of course. But you have to really believe it, believe it's a fact, an objective truth. You can't just manipulate your feelings and say, "I better believe this in order to get the feeling." Because that's not really believing it.

Sal: So I shouldn't look for good feelings in prayer— not even joy and peace and happiness.

Chris: Right. Just aim at God, the Giver, not the gifts.

Sal: And then the gifts will come.

Chris: Yes, but not as often as you'd like. We all have a spiritual sweet tooth, you know. Just as we like sweet foods, even though they're not as good for us, we like pleasant spiritual experiences, but all pleasure isn't good for us.

Pleasant spiritual experiences

Sal: But some is.

Chris: Yes.

Sal: And God gives us just the right amount for us?

Chris: Yes.

Sal: Even though it doesn't feel like it?

Chris: Yes. You catch on fast, Sal.

Sal: But I'm a little disappointed. I thought I was going to find a lot more joy in prayer. I thought it was really touching God, really experiencing him.

Chris: It is. And the joy you'll get in prayer is greater than any joy in the world. I guarantee you you'll never exchange it for anything. But it's not a steady diet. A meal isn't all dessert. A marriage isn't all honeymoon. The other parts are even more important for us, even though they don't feel as good.

Sal: I see.

Chris: Good. And do you see the connection between the two main things we said in this whole conversation: that the best prayer is the Lord's Prayer and that we should rely on faith in fact, not on feelings?

Sal: I think so. God's will, not ours, right?

Chris: Right.

Sal: I thought that principle was mainly for ethics, for living.

Chris: And what do you think prayer is? An escape from living and from the principles of living?

Sal: Oops.

Prayer is living.   *Chris:* It's just the opposite. It's a plunge into the very heart of living, the source of life, where the principles work with even greater force.

Sal: That's where I want to go: inside, to the center of all things.

Chris: That's great, Sal. Because "all who seek, find", remember?

Dialogue Four

The God You Pray to: What Difference Does Theology Make?

Sal: Well, what should we talk about today, Chris?

Chris: The same thing we talked about last time: fact.

Sal: What fact?

Chris: Let's look at the fact most relevant to prayer.

Sal: Great. And what is that?

Chris: The God we pray to, of course. Who he is.

Sal: Somehow it sounds strange to call God a "fact". Wouldn't "The Supreme Value" be better?

Chris: Certainly not! Don't you believe he's really there?   *God is a fact.*

Sal: Of course I do.

Chris: Then he's a fact.

Sal: I thought a fact was something you could prove scientifically.

Chris: Is it a fact that we're friends, or is that just fiction, or illusion, or fantasy?

Sal: It's a fact.

Chris: Can it be proved scientifically?

Sal: No. How can science measure friendship?

47

Chris: Then facts are more than what science can measure.

Sal: What are they?

Chris: Objective truths. Realities, independent of our ideas or our feelings.

Sal: It sounds so strange to call God a fact. Why should that be?

Chris: Because our civilization has reduced objective facts to what science can prove and has reduced God to a subjective fancy or feeling—or "value". What about you? Do you believe God is the Supreme Fact?

Sal: Yes. All right, God is the Supreme Fact.

Who is God?   *Chris:* Good. Now let's describe this Supreme Fact. Who is God?

Sal: I thought we were going to talk about prayer. This is theology.

Chris: We *are* going to talk about prayer. But prayer is talking with God. So we'd better know who this God is that we're talking to, right? How can you talk to someone if you don't know anything about him?

Sal: But we can't define God.

Chris: Who said anything about defining God? I just said "describe" him.

Sal: But what can we know about God, anyway? That's like a worm claiming to know what we are.

Chris: Yes, it is. We could never have figured out on our own who God is. But God has told us about himself.

Sal: Oh, yes. I forgot. How come that's so easy to forget?

Chris: Our whole civilization tends to forget it, even when it's being religious in its own way instead of God's way.

Sal: But not everything in theology is relevant to prayer, is it?

Chris: Of course it is. Because God's the one we pray to, remember?

Sal: All right, tell me how the doctrine of the Trinity is relevant to prayer.   *The Trinity*

Chris: That's easy. We need all three Persons of the Trinity, or else we can't pray.

Sal: How?

Chris: First, we need someone to pray *to*, right?

Sal: Of course.

Chris: That's the Father.

Sal: It's O.K. to pray to the Son or the Holy Spirit too, isn't it?

Chris: Of course.

Sal: And even to God as a whole, sort of? Without having a clear concept which person?

Chris: Yes. But ordinarily it's God the Father.

Sal: All right. Where do the other two come in?

Chris: The Son is the Way to the Father, the road we   *Jesus is the Way.*
walk along when we pray. He told us, "I am the way
. . . no one can come to the Father except through me." Do you believe that or not?

Sal: Of course I believe it.

Chris: It's not an "of course". It's one of his hard sayings. Not a whole lot of people believe that. Even a lot of Christians like to ignore it.

Sal: I think I see why. Does it mean that God doesn't hear the prayers of Jews and Hindus and Moslems and pagans?

Chris: No, it doesn't mean that. It means that he hears them through Jesus, if and when and how he hears them.

Sal: Oh. But they don't know Jesus.

Chris: But Jesus knows them.

Sal: O.K., what about the Holy Spirit?

Chris: He's the motive, the moving force, the energy, the inspiration inside us, the power to pray. We need him too.

Sal: You mean when we decide to pray, that's God the Holy Spirit moving us to want to pray?

Chris: Yes, and helping us to pray as we do it too.

Sal: That's a pretty big help—God himself!

Chris: Yes! God permeates us on all sides. God the Father is outside us. God the Son, Jesus, is God beside us. And God the Holy Spirit is God inside us. The Father is the home garage, the Son is the road, and the Holy Spirit is the car. Or the Holy Spirit is the fuel, the Son is the car, and the Father is the home we're driving to.

Sal: I see that—though I think you're getting carried away with your analogies. But I'm not as clear on the Holy Spirit and his role as I am on the Father and the Son. Why is that, do you think?

Chris: I think that's natural. The Holy Spirit is too close to us to see well, like the nose on your face. He's more like energy than like matter, or more like light than the object it illuminates. He's hard to objectify.

Sal: Is it really important, then, if you can't understand it as an object, if you can't objectify it?

Chris: Not "it", Sal; "him". He's a *person*—though not a human person, of course.

Sal: But why is he important?

Chris: Because he's like light. You can't see light itself, but without light, you can't see anything else. So you can't see him, even with your mind, but without him you can't see God the Father or God the Son. Only God can understand God. Only God can shine light on God.

Sal: So without the Holy Spirit, there can be no prayer.

Chris: Right.

Sal: Then every real prayer anybody ever prayed is inspired by the Holy Spirit?

Chris: In some way, yes. We don't always respond to that inspiration very well, but . . .

Sal: But that's awfully generous of him. To help people who don't even acknowledge his existence.

Chris: Yes. That's quite in character for God.

Sal: How do *you* know what's in character for God?

Chris: Same way you do. We've been told. Better, we've been shown.

Sal: Jesus, you mean?

Chris: Yes. He said, "No man has seen God at any time. The only begotten Son, he has made him known." Jesus is like a perfectly transparent window, with the Father shining through. He said, "I have come not to do my own will, but the will of my Father." He shows us and tells us what his Father is like—like the father of the prodigal son, he runs to meet us even after we've run away from him. So if you want to know what God the Father is like, look at Jesus. Jesus came to show us the Father, not himself.

Jesus shows us the Father.

Sal: But he showed us himself too, right? Because there's no difference.

Chris: No difference in *character*, in *nature*, right. But they're two different *persons*.

Sal: Sort of like twins?

Chris: Sort of, though that analogy fails when you push it.

Sal: But I thought they were different.

Chris: How?

Sal: I thought God the Father was stern and uptight about justice all the time, while Christ the Son was forgiving and merciful and loving.

Chris: That's a popular heresy today, just as it was over a thousand years ago. (It was called Gnosticism then.) No, Christ is just too, as well as loving, and the Father is loving too, as well as just. The Father is kind and forgiving too—haven't you read the Psalms? And the Son is stern too—haven't you read the Gospels?

Sal: O.K., so Jesus is like a window to the Father. Is the Holy Spirit like a window to Jesus, then?

Chris: Exactly. No one of them points to himself, puts himself forward. Even in the Trinity, each works for the other. That's why the basic law for our lives is to do the same thing. That's why unselfish love is our law; because it's the very life of our Creator. God is our model. Our ethics go all the way up.

Sal: That would have to be true. Otherwise God wouldn't practice what he preaches, or wouldn't preach what he practiced. So the reason we have to love is because God *is* love.

Chris: You see it very clearly, Sal. Yes. And do you also see how this very popular idea, that "God is love", is inseparable from another, much less popular idea, that God is a Trinity?

Love and the Trinity *Sal:* No. Why can't God be love without being a Trinity?

Chris: Because love is a relationship between more than one person. If God were only one person, he could still be a lover, but not love itself, not complete love itself. And then he wouldn't be unselfish love. He'd just be selfish love, loving himself eternally.

Sal: He could create *us* and love *us*.

Chris: Yes, but then he'd *have* to create us in order to love unselfishly. In himself, he'd just be selfish love. He'd depend on us, then, not us on him, for his unselfish love.

Sal: That certainly doesn't sound right—God depending on us. But this is theology; what difference does it make for prayer?

Chris: Your theology forms your prayer. Let's go through just the basic differences between theologies and see how they make a difference to prayer, all right? *Theology forms prayer.*

Sal: All right.

Chris: The first and most basic difference, of course, is between atheism and theism. If you're an atheist and believe there *is* no God, then you just don't pray, because there's no God to pray to.

Sal: Of course.

Chris: Then, within theism, the next distinction is between polytheism, belief in many gods, and monotheism, belief in one God. If you believe in many gods, you pray to many gods. That's like marrying many different partners. You split your allegiances and your loves. No one god is "all or nothing".

Sal: I see.

Chris: Then, within monotheism, there's a further distinction among three kinds of monotheism. First, pantheism. That's the belief that everything is God, and God is everything, that there's only one reality, and everything is it, or part of it. If you're a pantheist, you don't pray; you meditate and try to sink into this unity. You try realize your own divine identity. Because if everything is God, then you're God too. So you don't pray to an Other. *Pantheism*

Sal: I see. It looks like each theology does have a different kind of prayer. What other kinds of monotheism are there?

Chris: The opposite of pantheism is deism. Pantheism believes God is immanent but not transcendent—here and now but not distinct from the here and now, from the universe, not Other. Deism takes the opposite half: it believes God is far away and above the universe, but not present in it. According to the deist, God created the universe and then left it on its own, like winding *Deism* up a clock. So deists don't believe in miracles, or in the Incarnation.

Sal: How do deists pray?

Chris: They can worship God, as pantheists can't. But they can't ask him for anything. Their God doesn't answer prayers.

Sal: What's the third form of monotheism?

Chris: That God is both immanent and transcendent.

The God of the Bible

Sal: That's the God of the Bible, right?

Chris: Right. Jews and Moslems, as well as Christians, believe in this God. All three religions accept our Old Testament, and Christianity also accepts the New Testament, and Moslems add the Koran.

Sal: They all pray to the same God, then.

Chris: Yes, but Christians pray through Christ, because Christians are trinitarians. They believe God is a Trinity of persons, that Christ is one of them, that he is divine.

Sal: So Jews and Moslems are unitarians?

Chris: Yes.

Sal: I see how theology and prayer go together. I didn't realize theology made such a practical difference.

Chris: And now you see how it does.

Dialogue Five

The Dynamite
in Prayer

Sal: Well, Chris, what do we talk about today?

Chris: How about talking about dynamite?

Sal: Dynamite?

Chris: The dynamite in prayer.

Sal: Wow! What's that?

Chris: The Holy Spirit.

Sal: Oh . . .

Chris: You sound disappointed.

Sal: Well . . . you have to admit, "dynamite" is more of an attention-getter than "the Holy Spirit". I thought you were going to talk about something more . . . well, more practical.

Chris: I couldn't possibly do that, Sal.

Sal: Why not?

Chris: Because there's nothing more practical than the Holy Spirit.

Sal: Oh? What practical difference does it make, then?

Chris: Not "it", "he". He's a person, remember?

Sal: O.K. But what difference does he make? Or is that a wrong question to ask?

Chris: It's a very good question. If something makes no practical difference, no difference to your life, then you don't care about it. Who cares whether the moon has 1,000 or 2,000 craters on its dark side? Only astronomers. But we care about dynamite, if it's in our neighborhood. Because dynamite can make a difference, right?

Sal: Right. And the Holy Spirit can make as big a difference as dynamite?

Dynamite is power.

Chris: The Holy Spirit *is* dynamite. The word "dynamite" comes from one of the Greek words used in the New Testament to describe the Holy Spirit: *dynamis.* It means "power".

Sal: Oh, I think I understand. You mean unless there were a Holy Spirit, there couldn't be the power to start the Church and the power to inspire the writers of the Bible and so on. He's sort of like spiritual electricity?

Chris: That's part of it. But you seem disappointed again.

Sal: Because that's theoretical, theological. I want to know what practical difference he makes here and now. If he's spiritual electricity, I don't just want to know that he happens to be the source of power, I want to know if I can get a shock.

Chris: Good question. That's the other part of it, the practical difference he makes. Yes, you can get a shock. You can touch him.

Sal: He makes a difference, then. Good. But what difference?

Chris: The same kind of difference Jesus does. Just as Jesus gives you a new relationship with God the Father, the Holy Spirit gives you a new relationship with Jesus.

Sal: What new relationship?

Chris: There are a lot of aspects to it, but the heart of it is that Jesus becomes *real* to you, not just ideal or abstract. You *know* him, not just know *about* him. It's as big a change as Job found at the end of his story, when the God he had been praying to and complaining to and calling on finally came to him. When that happened, Job said, "I had heard of you with the hearing of the ear, but now I see you with the seeing of the eye." Firsthand knowing instead of secondhand. And that's as big a difference as . . . well, imagine your father had left home to fight in some foreign war when you were born, and you never saw him. You only got letters from him (that's like the Bible), and your mother told you about him (she's like the Church). Then one day he shows up at your front door and comes in, and you hug him and talk with him and play with him—you *meet* him.

Sal: I see. You mean the Holy Spirit brings Jesus home to me, sort of?

Bringing Jesus home

Chris: Exactly.

Sal: That *is* a tremendous difference.

Chris: Like the difference between a photograph and a person.

Sal: So the Holy Spirit makes Jesus more than just "thought about".

Chris: Yes.

Sal: More than "believed in" too? Beyond faith?

Chris: Not *beyond* faith, no; your faith *deepens*. It becomes more than an intellectual faith. You believe *in* Jesus, not just believe *things about* Jesus. You trust him. You get to know him, as you get to know a friend. By experience.

Sal: By feeling? Is that what you mean by "experience"?

Chris: No, not just feeling. Feeling is only a part of it. It's deeper than feeling, just as human love and human friendship is deeper than feelings. Feelings can change, but the relationship can endure. The feelings are only *in you*, but the relationship is *between* you and your friend. Feelings are subjective, but relationships are objective. The change the Holy Spirit makes is more than a subjective thing, a change in your feelings. It's a change in the real relationship between you and God.

Sal: And this is true about my prayer *and* about my life, right?

Chris: Right.

Sal: O.K., I think I see *where* the change is: in the relationship, not just in me. But I'm not clear *what* the change is.

The energy of God *Chris:* One part of it is that the action doesn't come only from you, but from God. The energy of God comes into your prayer and into your life.

Sal: Is that what the Holy Spirit is, "the energy of God"?

Chris: Yes, but remember, he's a Person, not just energy in the abstract.

Sal: But he's like electricity in that you can get a shock. You can touch him.

Chris: Yes. Actually, he touches you.

Sal: Not physically, of course?

Chris: No, but spirits can really touch too.

Sal: It sounds exciting. *He* sounds exciting. He must make prayer exciting.

Chris: Yes, but he doesn't give you a perpetual high. Remember, it's not primarily a matter of feeling. So even when you don't *feel* God is there, you still *know* he is.

Sal: With your mind?

Chris: No, it's more than intellectual, just as it's more than emotional. Deeper than both: the real presence of a person—a divine Person. All three of them, in fact.

Sal: It sounds incredibly precious.

Chris: It is. More precious than anything in this world. So precious that even if only one person who reads this book believes this one point and decides to ask God for the Holy Spirit (and everyone who asks, receives), then it will be infinitely worth all the time and effort of writing and publishing and distributing it to thousands of others, just for that one.

Sal: It sounds too good to be true, too good for me. I'm not good enough for it, I mean.

Chris: That's right. You're not. Nobody is. Nobody deserves God. God works by love, not justice. It's sheer grace, sheer gift. And he's free. He comes with the package deal. The Spirit comes with the Father and the Son.

Sal: Aren't there a lot of people who are living on only a third or two thirds of the package?

Chris: Yes! They're like the family of immigrants on a ship from Europe to America. They were so poor that they had to spend almost all their money on the ticket, and what they had left over for food was only enough to buy bread and cheese. So for the first couple of days all they ate was cheese sandwiches. Then the little boy said to his father, "Daddy, please, can I have money for an ice cream cone, just this once? I hate cheese sandwiches!" His father said, "We have almost no money left. And cheese sandwiches will keep you alive till we get to New York. Once we're there, there are golden streets and everybody's rich." The boy wouldn't stop asking, so his father finally gave him some change for an ice cream cone and waited. The boy didn't come back for two hours. His father was getting worried when the boy finally came back with a fat tummy and a smile on his face. "Did you get your ice cream cone?" "Oh, sure, Dad. And then another one, and then a steak, and then apple pie." "What? You bought all that with the money I gave you?" "Oh, no, Dad. It's free. It comes with the ticket!"

Cheese sandwiches

Sal: Ouch! I see the point. A lot of Christians are living on spiritual cheese sandwiches, and the Holy Spirit is steak, right?

Chris: Right. There's a passage in Acts where Paul goes into a church in Ephesus and asks the question: "Did you receive the Holy Spirit when you became believers?" And they answer, "Who's that? We never heard about the Holy Spirit." Why do you think Paul asked that question? I think he saw spiritual cheese instead of spiritual steak there. He sensed something missing: the power, the certainty, the joy. Maybe he'd ask the same question if he came to most of our churches.

Sal: This still sounds too good to be true. Are you sure it's for me? Not only for saints?

Chris: The Bible calls all Christians "saints".

Sal: Isn't it only for charismatics? Pentecostals? Holy Spirit people?

Chris: Don't let denominational lines and theological labels and walls of words keep you out. The Holy Spirit is for all Christians. That's very clear in the New Testament.

Baptism in the Holy Spirit

Sal: But this experience of him—the joy, the power, the certainty—is that what they call "the baptism in the Holy Spirit"?

Chris: That's what charismatics call it, yes, but it's not just for one group of Christians, not just for charismatics. In fact, that's just what charismatics say too.

Sal: You know, I've been impressed throughout these conversations of ours with how much solid substance there is in the Christianity common to all the different churches, Protestant and Catholic, charismatic and noncharismatic.

Chris: That's because I've tried to stick to the center.

Sal: The center?

Chris: God himself, Father, Son, and Holy Spirit. He's for everyone, not just one group. For all who will have him.

Sal: Are you saying denominational differences don't matter?

Chris: Not at all. The differences are very important. But even those very important differences can't compare with the deep agreement all Christians have about the center. We agree much more than we disagree.

Sal: Do all Christians agree about "the baptism in the Holy Spirit"?

Chris: No, but he's for everyone, whatever they think of him.

The Holy Spirit is for everyone.

Sal: Is "the baptism in the Holy Spirit" necessary for salvation?

Chris: No. Steak isn't necessary for food either; cheese sandwiches will keep you alive. But when the steak is free, why not take it?

Sal: I thought the Holy Spirit was given to everybody who's saved, everyone who's a Christian. Didn't Jesus promise the Holy Spirit to all his disciples?

Chris: Yes, he did. The "baptism in the Holy Spirit" isn't the same as Christ giving us the Holy Spirit in the first place. The Holy Spirit is given to us as soon as we believe.

Sal: What's the "baptism in the Spirit" then?

Chris: A release of the power of the Spirit who's already there.

Sal: O.K., that point is cleared up. But I'm still not clear how you know the "baptism in the Spirit" is for all Christians, just as the giving of the Spirit in the first place is. Only a few seem to have it.

Chris: Because when it first happened, on Pentecost, Peter said to the thousands there, who heard the mighty wind and saw the tongues of fire and heard the apostles speaking in tongues, "Repent, and be

Acts 2 is for us too.

baptized every one of you in the name of Jesus Christ for the forgiveness of your sins, and you shall receive the gift of the Holy Spirit"—that's the three parts of the Christian package deal: repentance to the Father, salvation by the Son *and* receiving the Holy Spirit. Peter then went on to say that "the promise (the whole promise, including the Holy Spirit) is to you and to your children and to all that are far off, every one whom the Lord our God calls". It's as if Peter was looking down the centuries, over the heads of his listeners, and saw us, and said to us, "This is for you too." Look; it makes sense. God is love, and what's the gift a lover longs most to give? What do flowers or a wedding ring symbolize?

Sal: The lover himself. The gift of self.

Chris: So God wants to give each one of us himself, his *whole* self, Father *and* Son *and* Holy Spirit. God is pure love, pure generosity, and the aim of love is always intimacy, oneness with the beloved. Doesn't the lover always want to get closer and closer, to get inside the beloved's soul? You want to give your whole self to the one you love. That's why God gave us the Holy Spirit. And that's why it's better to have the Holy Spirit than to have Jesus only physically present, as the first disciples did.

Sal: Better even than having Jesus here on earth?

Why "it is better that I go away." *Chris:* Yes, that's what he said himself. He said, "It is better for you that I go away (he was speaking of his ascension into Heaven) because if I do not go away, the Spirit will not come to you, but if I go away, I will send him to you."

Sal: Why is that?

Chris: Because no matter how close you are to Jesus, without the Holy Spirit, Jesus is still somebody outside you. He's close *beside* you, but the Holy Spirit is *inside* you. That's even closer, and that's what love wants, remember: closeness.

Sal: You mean we're really better off now without Jesus, with the Holy Spirit instead?

Chris: No, no, not "instead". Jesus is with us too. He promised that: "Behold, I am with you always, even unto the end of the world." The Holy Spirit is *his* Spirit. The Holy Spirit reveals *Jesus* to us.

Sal: But we're better off without Jesus' bodily presence? Better off after Jesus' ascension into Heaven than before?

Chris: Yes.

Sal: That's pretty hard to believe. Frankly, I should think it would be fantastic if we could talk to him now, directly.

Chris: Ah, but you can!

Sal: Oh. Prayer, you mean?

Chris: Yes. *Because* Jesus sent us his Spirit instead of leaving us his human body, our prayers can be more intimate.

Sal: How?

Chris: You *know* the one you talk to. He's your friend, not a stranger. And he talks back, and you hear him. Not usually in words . . . we'll talk later about that. And here's another difference he makes: he lights up Scripture. When you read it, it's not a dead book, but alive.

The Holy Spirit and Scripture

Sal: What do you mean by that? It sounds pretty vague.

Chris: What's the difference between a love letter and an encyclopedia?

Sal: I see: the first one is alive.

Chris: And the whole Bible becomes a love letter written to you personally, not some old, historical encyclopedia.

Sal: To me personally?

Chris: Yes. God doesn't address his mail "Dear Occupant".

Sal: You can really see that big of a difference in the way you read the Bible?

Chris: Yes. *It* reads *you* now. It becomes like a sword: not dead on the ground, but alive because Somebody's hand is using it.

Sal: That Somebody is the Holy Spirit?

Chris: Yes. The Bible calls itself "the Sword of the Spirit", you know.

Sal: It sounds almost scary.

Chris: It can be—like looking through a keyhole and seeing an eye looking back at you. But it's the eye of Infinite Love. Here's another way to put the difference it makes: Did you ever see one of those kids' puzzles in the Sunday papers, where there's a jungle scene or something, and the puzzle reads, "Find the man in the picture"? After you squint and turn it sideways you notice that that tree trunk is his mouth, and that elephant ear is his chin, and so on. Then, once you see all the lines as part of his face, you can never see that picture the same again. It's not just a jungle; it's a man. It's a little like seeing the "man in the moon". But in the case of Scripture, he's really there—though he's not just a man, he's God. Every word becomes part of his face, tells you about *him*. You meet *him* now when you read.

Sal: Really? You're not exaggerating or idealizing?

Chris: No. It really happens.

Sal: That's a way to pray, then: reading Scripture.

Chris: Yes. We'll talk about that later too.

Sal: And I suppose the Holy Spirit makes a difference to your life too, right?

The Holy Spirit and guidance *Chris:* Of course. One difference is that he gives you a sense of direction, of guidance. You need more than written rules, you know.

Sal: Why?

Chris: Because no set of rules can cover everything. Situations and personalities are different. There *are* rules, but we have to apply them to different situations. That's where the Holy Spirit helps. You sense what his will is because you know him—just as you can tell what your father would want you to do in a situation because you know him. But you don't know what some stranger would want you to do, because you just don't know him personally.

Sal: O.K., enough! It's for me. What do I do? How do I get it?

How to get the Holy Spirit

Chris: Only ask.

Sal: That's all?

Chris: That's all.

Sal: No, that can't be. It's too simple, too easy. What's the catch?

Chris: No catch.

Sal: What are my chances?

Chris: Chances?

Sal: Of getting all these great things you described.

Chris: Oh, 100 percent.

Sal: Can you prove that?

Chris: I sure can. Read Luke 11. . . . Here it is. Don't believe me; believe Jesus. Here's what he says: "I say to you, ask and it will be given to you; seek, and you will find; knock and it will be opened to you. For everyone who asks receives, and he who seeks finds, and to him who knocks it will be opened."

Sal: How can it be that simple? And how do you know that Jesus was talking about the Holy Spirit in that passage?

Chris: He himself answers both of those questions in the next few verses: "If a son asks for bread from any father among you, will he give him a stone? Or if he

Ask and you will receive.

asks for a fish, will he give him a serpent instead of a fish? Or if he asks for an egg, will he offer him a scorpion? If you then, being evil, know how to give good gifts to your children, how much more will your heavenly Father give the Holy Spirit to those who ask him!"

Sal: Just "those who ask"? That's all it says?

Chris: That's all.

Sal: It's just too good to be true.

Chris: If it isn't true, Jesus is a liar. Isn't that even harder to believe?

Sal: Of course, but maybe we're misinterpreting his words.

Chris: How much clearer and simpler could they be? In fact, it's *too* simple for you! That's your objection: "It just can't be that simple." But it is. Love is very simple-hearted. It just loves to give gifts, just because it's love. That's what God is: just love.

Sal: I think love just trapped me in a corner. And I don't want to escape.

Dialogue Six

Five Reasons to Pray When You Don't Want To

Sal: Chris, I'm having a hard time praying.

Chris: Any special reason why?

Sal: Yes. I find I just don't have much to say to God. Isn't that awful?

Chris: No, it's quite normal.

Sal: Do you feel that way too?

Chris: Sometimes.

Sal: When I *do* have things to say, it goes along naturally and spontaneously, but . . .

Chris: Tell me how it goes when it *does* go well, when you do have plenty to say.

Sal: Well, I say whatever I feel. God's my closest friend. I can tell him anything, because I know he never misunderstands me or puts me down, as people do sometimes. That's why I can be completely open with him and why it's hard to be completely open to people. I just tell him everything.

Chris: Great!

Sal: But sometimes "everything" isn't much. Then what? Sometimes "everything" doesn't even last five minutes.

Chris: So you wonder what to do then.

Sal: Yes. Any suggestions?

Chris: Hmmm. . . . Yes. Three of them. The first we talked about before: just be silent and listen to him instead of talking.

Sal: You'll have to tell me how to do that sometime.

Using formal prayers *Chris:* Yes. Soon. The second thing is to use formal prayers, written prayers.

Sal: That feels a little artificial to me.

Chris: Why?

Sal: Well, I wouldn't read a written conversation to someone I love.

Chris: Would you sing a written song to someone you love?

Sal: Sure.

Chris: Well, written prayers are like songs. That's why they're more formal and poetic. That's also why they're usually old, like a lot of great songs. Millions have used them and loved them and been helped by them. They've stood the test of time; that's why they're still around. The Church uses them and offers them to us like the master of a big, old house who pulls out of his storehouse things old and new.

Sal: That sounds familiar.

Chris: Jesus said it.

Sal: But don't we need the new more than the old? I mean our own ad-lib prayers more than the Church's old ones?

Chris: We need both. If we had only the old formal prayers and never talked to God spontaneously, the relationship would be cold and impersonal and distant. But if we use only our own spontaneous prayers, we miss out on jewels. And we run into your problem of what to say next.

Sal: But didn't Jesus ridicule the Pharisees for using long formal prayers?

Chris: No; for not meaning them, for praying with the lips but not the heart. But he never said to pray with the heart and *not* the lips. If Jesus didn't want us to use set prayers, then he set a very bad example, because when his disciples asked him, "Teach us to pray", he gave them—he gave *us*—the Lord's Prayer. And he and his disciples constantly used the Psalms, which are formal prayers. Even dying on the cross, he quoted a Psalm.

Sal: Didn't he say we should pray in the Spirit?

Chris: We can pray these formal prayers in the Spirit. We don't just recite prayers, we pray; just as we don't just recite songs, we sing. Just because someone else wrote the words, that doesn't mean we can't make them our own and mean them from the heart. You should know that. Your own church uses them. Most churches do.

Praying in the Spirit

Sal: I guess I never made them my own. And I guess there's no reason I can't. Do you have any advice on how to pray formal prayers like the Lord's Prayer and the Psalms?

Chris: Yes, but let's set aside our next conversation for that. My third answer to your question of what to do when you run out of things to say to God is going to take some time.

Sal: What is it?

Chris: Besides listening and using formal prayers, you could remember the five reasons to pray.

Five reasons to pray

Sal: What are they?

Chris: Christians throughout the ages have found five kinds of things to say to God, five reasons to pray. The traditional names for them are Adoration, Confession, Thanksgiving, Intercession, and Petition.

Sal: Should every prayer contain all five?

Chris: Not necessarily. Any one is a good reason to pray. But all five are even better.

Sal: What are they again? I've forgotten already.

Chris: Adoration, Confession, Thanksgiving, Intercession, and Petition. A.C.T.I.P., if you want to remember them that way. The tip of the act, the five points of the act of prayer. Think of prayer as a star, with five points.

Sal: Let's go through them one by one.

Adoration   *Chris:* O.K. The basic point of each is very simple, but you can pray endless variations on each one. First, adoration. It means worship, of course. Absolute respect. Acknowledging that God is God: unique, perfect, absolute, infinite, totally worthy of all our praise and all our love.

Sal: Is this a matter of the mind or the heart?

Chris: Both. The mind sees it, and the heart sings it, shouts it: "Alleluia!"—which means "Praise God!" or "Hurrah for God!" "Praise the Lord!" is the formula many Christians use. Adoration is what we should give only to God, total and uncritical.

Sal: Uncritical?

Chris: Certainly. Naïve, accepting, like a little child. Would you be God's critic?

Becoming   *Sal:* I guess that's foolish. Is that what Jesus meant
like a child   when he said, "Unless you become as a little child, you cannot enter the Kingdom of heaven"?

Chris: I think that's part of it, yes.

Sal: Little children don't think about themselves much. Is that part of it too? Being unself-conscious?

Chris: Yes. If you're self-conscious, you do it for yourself; if you're unself-conscious, you just think about God, you do it for God's sake.

Sal: But he doesn't need our prayers. What do you mean, "for God's sake"?

Chris: He doesn't need our prayers, no, but he deserves them. I mean our motive for adoring God should be simply to give him what he deserves.

Sal: And what's that?

Chris: Adoration. Our whole heart and soul and mind and strength. That's his first and greatest commandment, Jesus tells us.

Sal: So it's to obey his commandment.

Chris: Also to live in reality. The reason to adore God is to be honest, to be true, to live according to what's real. God is really adorable; that's the fundamental reason to adore him: to live in the real world. *What is the real world?*

Sal: Most people mean something quite different by "reality" or "the real world", you know.

Chris: Then they must be pagans or atheists, if their god is less real than whatever they mean by reality.

Sal: I think they mean headaches and income tax and traffic jams.

Chris: Yes, and that's why they get so upset about them: they think they're more real than God.

Sal: I see: adoring God makes a real difference to our lives, then. I mean, when we're in a traffic jam, if we've been in the habit of adoring God, we'll have a more realistic perspective on it. Little things won't seem big and big things little.

Chris: You *do* see.

Sal: I'm not sure of one thing, though: Does God need our prayers or not?

Chris: No, he doesn't need them, but he wants them. Like a father, he doesn't need his baby's hugs or his teenager's birthday cards, but he wants them.

Sal: I see. Adoration is love.

Chris: Yes, and we mustn't think God commands us to love and adore him as some tyrant would, or some egotist who needs people's praises to flatter his ego. God doesn't need adoration like a tyrant; he prescribes it like a doctor.

Sal: It's for us, then, not for him.

Chris: God's motive in commanding it is for us, yes. But our motive in doing it is for him, because he wants it; he wants our love.

Sal: Why?

Chris: Because he loves us. What does any lover want from the one loved?

Sal: Love.

God wants our love.

Chris: Yes. Freely given. In loving and adoring God we give him the one thing he can't give himself: our free love.

Sal: You said that once before.

Chris: I hope I'll remember to say it many times again. It's worth remembering. For both of us. For everybody.

Sal: Oh, that explains it. . . .

Chris: Explains what?

Sal: Something else I was going to ask you about adoring God: why it doesn't get boring if you just repeat it over and over. But it's like two lovers saying "I love you" to each other over and over, isn't it?

Chris: It *is* two lovers saying "I love you" to each other over and over. That's exactly what the prayer of adoration is.

Sal: You mean that's not just a metaphor?

Chris: No. The Bible says, "God *is* love", remember?

Sal: And God talks back to us? He says, "I love you" to us too?

Chris: Yes. We have to learn to listen and hear him. We'll talk about that part of it soon, some other time.

Sal: I just realized something else. If love is the greatest thing in the world, then the prayer of love is the greatest prayer in the world. No wonder it's not boring. But if you're not in love with God, it sure is boring. Imagine saying "I love you" over and over to someone you don't care about!

Chris: Saying it over and over isn't the only way to adore, either. Just *being* there, without words; just sitting, gazing into each other's face—isn't that what lovers want to do? Isn't that what they're perfectly content with?

Sal: Yes. But how does that analogy work for God? We don't see God face to face, as we see the ones we love in this world.

Chris: No; the gaze is by faith, not sight. The inner eye, not the outer ones.

Sal: Then that makes it harder than human love, because in human love you see the beloved.

Chris: That's right. That's why God gave us the easy *Learning to love* lessons first, the lessons in human love—not just romantic love, but friendship and affection and brotherly love—all kinds of natural human loves are training for divine love. For "if you don't love your brother, whom you have seen, how can you love God, whom you have not seen?"

Sal: That's quite a jump, though, from us to God, from loving people you see to loving God, whom you don't see.

Chris: But love is love, however different its objects. Little children sometimes learn to love people by loving pets first. There's a tremendous difference between animals and people, but loving animals can be training

for loving people. So human loves give us some training for loving God. But we love God with total love:
adoration. No human being deserves total adoration,
any more than an animal deserves human love.

Sal: I see; however different the steps on the ladder,
it's one ladder of love, and it ends in God.

Chris: Yes. Or, to put it differently, God is like the
sun, and all loves are like sunbeams received into
the atmosphere, lighting up a little of our world.
Sunbeams are made of the same stuff as the sun, but
far away and tiny. So human loves are made of what
God is made of, but only tiny and remote bits of it.

Sal: Adoring God pays off for us, too, doesn't it?

Chris: What do you mean?

Sal: I mean, it's for God, but it gives us joy. Like a
cheer at a football game: it's for the team, but it also
makes us feel good.

Forgetting yourself   *Chris:* Yes. That's its by-product. But try to make
that its product, and it won't work. I mean, if you
make your own happiness your motive for adoring
God, then you're not really adoring God, and then
it won't make you happy. You have to forget yourself
and your happiness; only then will you be happy.

Sal: That sounds like a paradox.

Chris: It is. But it's true. Aren't you happiest when
you're so caught up in something great that you forget
yourself?

Sal: Yes, you're right.

Chris: When we forget our troubles and ourselves
and just look at God and love God, it's a foretaste
of heaven. Do you think we'll be worrying about
ourselves there when there's *God* to look at?

Sal: Not unless God is smaller than we are! Or unless
we're fools.

Chris: And when we practice that principle of heavenly self-forgetfulness here and now, things begin happening in our lives. Our troubles often get taken care of somehow, or turn out to be blessings in disguise, or at least get smaller, as God gets bigger. God crowds out the dust and dirt in our lives.

Sal: And I guess if we're going to do it in heaven, we'd better practice here, we'd better get used to it, right?

Chris: Right. A very practical point.

Sal: It's best to *start* prayer with adoration, isn't it? Before the other four things?

Start with adoration.

Chris: Yes, because it puts you in the right frame of mind for everything else. Confession, for instance.

Sal: How?

Chris: After you're in God's presence adoring him and his greatness, you understand your littleness. After you realize his holiness, you realize your sinfulness. "In Thy light we see light", says the Psalm. Measured by human standards, you're probably pretty good. You live up to what other people expect of you. But by God's standards we all fall short.

Sal: That's awfully negative.

Chris: It's what God says: "All have sinned and come short of the glory of God."

Sal: What does that mean, the "glory of God"?

Chris: The glory he designed us for: his own. He wants us to share his perfections. That's why the saints seem so extreme about sin, why they say they're the worst of sinners: they're judging by God's standards, not man's.

Sal: I always wondered about that. Isn't that extremism a little sick?

Chris: Not if it's true! Do you think the great saints see *less* deeply into themselves than we do? Do you think we're right and they're wrong when we see ourselves as pretty good, and they see themselves as pretty bad? Is sanctity a sickness? An illusion?

Sal: I certainly don't want to believe that. But *why* not? What's the proof?

Hooked on sin **Chris:** God's Word, for one thing. It tells us some very bad news—that we're all habitual sinners, hooked on sin—before it tells us the good news, that God loves us anyway and saves us from sin. Doctor God tells us the diagnosis before the cure, the disease before the healing. Otherwise, why go to a doctor, if you don't have a serious disease?

Sal: Jesus said that, didn't he?

Chris: Yes: "Those who are well have no need of a physician, but those who are sick. . . . For I did not come to call the righteous, but sinners, to repentance."

Sal: You get a lot of your ideas from him, don't you?

Chris: Thank you, yes. I take that as high praise. But look, here's a second piece of evidence for thinking the saints are not sick or foolish when they say they're great sinners—a piece of evidence in them, not in the Bible, so that even someone who doesn't believe the Bible has to be impressed with it. It's their joy, their peace, their sense of freedom.

Sal: Yes, how do you explain that? If they're so down on themselves, you'd expect them to be gloomy, not full of joy.

God's forgiveness **Chris:** The solution to that puzzle is that their confession of sin takes place in the context of their adoration of God. *God*—the same God whose light tells them the truth of their sin—gives them that joy and peace and freedom by his forgiveness and love. You see, the more you adore God, the more you get to know him. And the great saints know him as both infinitely just *and* infinitely loving, holy *and* merciful, uncompromising *and* forgiving, demanding *and* compassionate, hard to please but easy to satisfy—like a good father.

(Jesus knew what to call him!) So they don't try to make excuses or minimize sin or get away with anything. But they also know God forgives all their sins because Christ died for them.

Sal: I see. It's quite simple, really.

Chris: And another reason for beginning prayer with adoration.

Sal: Hmm. Adoration is the most basic and essential form of prayer then, isn't it?

Chris: Yes. Most of the liturgical prayers of almost all churches are praise. There's more praise in the Psalms than anything else.

Sal: It sounds right to put praising God ahead of asking God for things. But isn't that like putting poetry ahead of prose, or song ahead of speech?

Chris: Yes, it is. Who ever said prose was more important than poetry, or speech more important than song? Some people's lives seem all prose and no poetry, no song; nose to the grindstone, no lifting up the eyes and the spirit to heaven. That's not the way to live, is it?

Sal: No. I guess we don't sing much, we Americans, do we? We let our paid professionals do it for us most of the time.

Chris: Well, let's not make the same mistake in prayer. Let's sing a lot.

Sal: Literally?

Chris: Why not? But even if you don't sing literally, praise is like singing compared with the rest of prayer.

Sal: Well, let's get on to the prose. Confession next, *Confession* right? What is confession?

Chris: Just what it says: confessing our sins and repenting, turning away from them, leaving our spiritual garbage at the feet of Jesus the garbage man.

Sal: Isn't that language a little disrespectful?

Chris: Ever look at a crucifix?

Sal: Of course . . .

Chris: Well, what's more disrespectful, a garbage man or a criminal executed by hanging on a cross?

Sal: I see. So Jesus is our garbage man.

Chris: And we put our garbage out each day by a simple and sincere and honest confession and repentance.

Sal: Of every little sin?

Dangers in confession

Chris: Of everything we remember, anything bothering us, any way we know or think we disobeyed God. There are two mistakes to avoid here: having nothing to confess and having too much, having no conscience and having too scrupulous a conscience, worrying too much about sin. I know we all need confession, but I think it should be the shortest of the five parts of prayer. Too much introspection is bad for the soul; you get ingrown eyeballs. That's why it's better to start with adoring God and forgetting yourself than to start with confession of sins; we should look at God more and ourselves less.

Sal: Why is too much introspection bad for us?

Chris: Because it leads to one of three traps: either we think we're just fine, and become arrogant, smug, self-satisfied, and self-righteous; or else we think we're terrible and become worried and miserable and plagued by guilt; or else we compromise and think of ourselves as not terribly good *or* terribly bad, and then we think of ourselves as dull, wishy-washy nothings, which is worst of all. We *are* very good (but not the way the self-righteous person thinks) *and* very bad (but not the way the person with a guilt complex thinks).

Sal: And the way out of that trap is just not to ask the question how well we're doing spiritually?

Chris: Oh, we should take our spiritual temperature once in a while, especially when we fear we're getting sick, contracting some new spiritual disease. But let's not be hypochondriacs, staring at the thermometer or (worse) at ourselves all the time. When we've sinned, the thing to do is to bring that garbage to the Savior and leave it there, not to keep rooting around in it.

Sal: That sounds healthy. O.K., what's the next point? Thanksgiving, isn't it? *Thanksgiving*

Chris: Yes. Counting your blessings. Thanking God for life's little pleasures and big graces. You can spend a long time on this one too, and it does you a lot of good, as well as being right and fitting to reality. God deserves to be thanked a lot.

Sal: Sounds similar to adoration. How is it different?

Chris: In adoration you love and adore God for what he is. In thanksgiving, you thank him for his gifts to you.

Sal: Is it good to make a list?

Chris: Sure!

Sal: You know, I don't feel grateful much of the time.

Chris: You can still be grateful even though you don't feel it.

Sal: How can that be?

Chris: You can still believe God is good to you and choose to thank him, *will* to thank him for his gifts. Neither faith nor thanksgiving depend on feelings.

Sal: But feelings sure help.

Chris: Yes, but prayers without their help are even more important, more valuable, like walking without crutches. I think God prizes much more the prayers we make without being helped by our feelings. *Praying without feelings*

Sal: Why? Just because they're harder?

Chris: No, because they're more truly ours, our free choice.

Sal: What's wrong with feelings?

Chris: Nothing, of course. All I'm saying is this: what we freely choose comes from us, from within. What we feel comes partly from without. Our emotions are influenced by the weather, our health, and a thousand other things. We're not wholly responsible for them. So when we pray when we feel like it, we're not sure how much we're praying only *because* we feel like it. But when we pray when we don't feel like it, then we know we're praying because we freely chose to.

Sal: I see. So I should pray even if praying doesn't seem to make any difference to my feelings, doesn't make me feel any better.

Chris: Yes, because the reason to pray isn't your happiness, but God's worthiness, God's glory. God deserves your adoration and gratitude even if you don't feel like giving them to him. Do you agree?

Sal: Yes. But God gave us feelings too, didn't he? To help?

Chris: Yes. We're children, learning to walk, and it's good for us to have and use the walkers God gave us, and even to ask for them when we don't have them. Sometimes God will give them, sometimes not, just like a parent with a toddler.

Count your blessings. *Sal:* Making a list of my blessings, "counting my blessings", will make me feel grateful, I suppose. But isn't that manipulating my feelings?

Chris: No, it's not faking anything, just honestly looking at reality, being realistic, fitting your feelings to reality. For instance, look at your feet.

Sal: My feet?

Chris: Yes. Think what wonderful and effective machines they are. Thank God for two healthy feet. Some people don't have them, you know. Did you ever hear the saying, "I felt bitter about having no shoes until I saw a man who had no feet"?

Sal: I don't think I'd feel grateful at that. We deserve to have two feet and even two shoes.

Chris: No, we don't. How could we? Our very life is a gift. We weren't even there to deserve it before we were conceived. If we don't deserve our very existence, then everything is gift.

Sal: Everything is gift?

Chris: From God, yes. Grass, potatoes, pigs, time, fire, water, stars, sheep for wool and wool for clothes and clothes for beauty and beauty itself—everything is gift. The Bible says, "In *everything* give thanks." The list is endless when we start counting our blessings. Try it. You'll like it. Gratitude heals many wounds.

Sal: It seems to make you smaller—humbler.

Chris: Bigger too. Humility seems to make you small but it really expands you, frees you. Pride seems to make you bigger, but it really makes you small and narrow and hard and brittle and full of hangups.

Sal: I guess you're right.

Chris: Don't be so easily convinced.

Sal: What do you mean? You're not sure yourself?

Chris: I am. But you shouldn't believe it just because I say so. You should demand to find out for yourself by experiment, by experience. Remember, talking about praying is like talking about cooking or singing. It's no good unless you *do* it.

Sal: O.K., but I want to know *what* to do first. What's the fourth purpose of prayer?

Chris: Intercession. Praying for others. *Intercession*

Sal: That's certainly practical.

Chris: It's also powerful. Even if you don't see the results, we're assured that no prayer is unheard, unanswered, or unused. "More things are wrought by prayer than this world dreams of." You can help save the world from a hospital bed or a wheelchair. You can do more by prayer than by anything else.

Sal: More than by anything else? Why is that?

Chris: Think of your life as a series of concentric circles, with yourself at the center. The people you meet every day—your family and close friends—are near you, and you touch them directly, by words and deeds. Then there is the outer circle of people; you rarely touch them directly, but indirectly, through other people. A word or an act of love to a friend might help him to help *his* friend, for instance. Then, you can influence people you never meet by writing letters, or doing good work. Think how many people were satisfied with the tables that came out of Joseph's carpenter shop. Then you can make an even broader difference as a citizen; your personal vote influences the whole state, the whole country. Finally, in prayer your vote reverberates throughout the universe, because it bounces off God. Prayer is the widest circle of influence we have. It can encompass everything. It can make a difference to anything.

Sal: I should spend a lot of time at intercession, then.

Chris: Yes. And it's a good idea to keep a list of people and needs to pray for and not to stop until your prayers are answered. Remember Jesus' parable about the persistent woman and the unjust judge.

Sal: O.K., and what's the fifth purpose of prayer?

Petition   *Chris:* Petition. Praying for your own needs.

Sal: Is the sky the limit here too?

Chris: Yes, but if you're honest with yourself, you'll ask yourself first whether what you want is what you need, and then ask God only for what you honestly believe you need. Jesus told us to pray, "Give us this day our daily bread", not "give us this day our daily spices." God will give us some spices, some extras, but we're told to ask for our needs.

Sal: If adoration is the highest form of prayer, this is the lowest, right? Shouldn't we minimize it? Wouldn't it be better just to praise and thank God and not to ask for anything at all?

Chris: God himself commanded us to ask him for things. It's like a father telling his children, "Come to me when you need lunch money." We do have needs, and God wants us to use them as another opportunity to come to him. We shouldn't abandon a road God himself has made for us.

Sal: Why did he make it at all? If he can give us anything we need at any time, why did he tell us to pray for it?

Why ask for things?

Chris: To give us the dignity of being causes.

Sal: What does that mean?

Chris: That's how Pascal put it. He means, we share the work. We count. Just like physical work: God could have given us everything without us working for it, but he knew it was better for us to work for things. The same with prayer.

Sal: I see. Is that why God sometimes doesn't give us a thing, even if it's good for us, until we pray a lot for it?

Chris: Yes, because he sees that we need prayer even more than we need the things we pray for, just as your body needs exercise more than it needs to reach the finish line of a race. Aiming for the line helps you to exercise. God wants us to persist in praying, even to the point of being pesty, like the lady in Jesus' parable who kept bothering the unjust judge until he granted her request.

Sal: Jesus likened God to an unjust judge?

Chris: The point of the parable is that if even an unjust human judge is moved by persistence in petitioning him, how much more will our just and loving heavenly Father?

Sal: So God hears all prayers.

Chris: Yes.

God answers all prayers. *Sal:* And answers them?

Chris: Yes. And sometimes the answer is No, when he sees that the thing we ask for, the thing that seems good to us, isn't really good for us. And sometimes the answer is Wait, when he sees that it's better for us to get it later rather than sooner. And sometimes the answer is Yes, right now, or very soon. But even "very soon"—like tomorrow—is a little "Wait". And a wait of fifty years is only a little more of the same thing, waiting. Even a lifetime, even "not till heaven", is only more of the same answer ,"Wait". So we have to learn to wait for God and trust his timing. But he always gives us what's good for us. Every good thing we ask for, we get, sooner or later.

Sal: Everything?

Chris: That's what Jesus said.

Sal: That's incredible!

Chris: No, it's reasonable, even inevitable, if God is all power, all wisdom, and all love. Because love wants to give us all good, and wisdom plans the best time schedule for it and the best way to give it, and power is able to do what love wants and wisdom plans. So Jesus' incredible promise that the Father will grant *all* our real desires, that whatever we ask for we will receive— this is reasonable if God is all love, all wisdom, and all power. In fact, if we *didn't* eventually get everything we need, everything that's really good for us, then there would have to be a deficiency either in God's love or wisdom or power. Either he wouldn't want to give us good, or he wouldn't know how, or he wouldn't be able to. So if we believe in the God of infinite goodness, wisdom, and power, we can ask in total confidence of receiving.

Sal: That sounds too good to be true.

Chris: Can you disprove it?

Sal: No, but isn't there some catch?

Is there a catch?

Chris: No, just the need to believe and wait.

Sal: Don't we have to be saints and have great faith?

Chris: All Christians are saints, and all Christians have faith.

Sal: How much faith do we have to have?

Chris: Faith isn't fundamentally a "how much" thing, like a feeling. It's an either-or thing. Do you believe in the God Jesus revealed or not? The infinitely loving, wise, and powerful Creator and Savior?

Sal: I do.

Chris: Then you can be sure you'll get every good thing you pray for. So be very careful what you pray for; God takes you more seriously than you take him sometimes.

Sal: Everything! Wow. . . .

Chris: In God's time and God's way.

God's time and God's way

Sal: I think I understand God's time, but what's God's way?

Chris: Let's just see whether you understand God's time first. Suppose you're praying for a healing from sickness, and God doesn't give it to you. Suppose he lets you suffer. What do you think is happening?

Sal: Either God's timing is off or mine is, so I guess it must be mine. For some reason I don't understand, God sees that it would be better for me to wait for my healing.

Chris: Good. But suppose you die of the disease?

Sal: Then I get healed in heaven. Nobody's sick there. So I really get what I need eventually—eternally, in fact. I'll never be sick again.

Chris: Good answer. You see that God's timing isn't always ours. Now let's look at "God's *way*". Suppose you pray for peace on earth, and God lets a terrible war happen instead. That might be God's way to peace, the best or the only way to destroy the power of a bully or an aggressor. Or suppose your country is fighting a war you believe is just and you pray for victory, and God gives you, instead, a peace treaty full of compromises. What you're fighting for and praying for is peace, isn't it? The only reason for fighting a war is to stop war —like building backfires, little brush fires at the edge of a forest to burn a few trees out and stop a great raging forest fire by depleting its fuel. So God's way of giving you your need in both cases—peace—wasn't your way. You may not want to fight for it, and God may make you fight for it. Or you may want to fight for it, and God may not. And that applies to all kinds of fighting, all kinds of effort, not just military.

Sal: I see. God always gives you the goods, but not always by the route you ask for. I understand. He's got the road map. But he seems to be just sitting by the side of the road a lot of the time, not moving. There's so much that needs to be done to clean up this world. Why isn't he doing more?

Chris: Maybe he's waiting for us, both to work and to pray. There's so much evil in the world partly because so few people pray. We can help save the world by prayer, you know. Remember in Genesis how one man's prayer—Abraham, it was—almost saved two cities, Sodom and Gomorrah? And Moses' prayer did save all the Jews from destruction, in Exodus.

Prayer changes things.

Sal: So it's true that "prayer changes things".

Chris: It sure is! Some paralytic in a hospital bed may be one of the most important people in the world. God may be saving the world from nuclear war because of such prayers.

Sal: Can one person make that big a difference?

Chris: One vote can win an election. Every vote counts. Every prayer counts. In war, every weapon counts, every bullet counts. And prayer is spiritual warfare.

Sal: I don't like that military metaphor.

Chris: Then blame Saint Paul, not me. But he makes clear that "we do not wrestle against flesh and blood, but against principalities and powers . . . against the spiritual hosts of wickedness in the heavenly places." It's a real war, and the whole universe is the battlefield. But the most important battlefield is our own souls.

Sal: Spiritual warfare—that makes prayer more than just a good thing to do. That makes it a necessity, a duty, an assignment, like a spy mission.

Chris: Yes. We should make a prayer list—a list of friends and needs to pray for—and treat it like a spy's assignment each morning, a map of enemy-infiltrated territory for us to conquer. And a map is not just to read, but to follow. So let's go. Let's do it. Let's stop talking and start praying.

The Three Greatest Things in the World

Chris: Say, Sal, I've been thinking about another answer to the question you asked me last time, about what to say to God, what kinds of things to say in prayer. I remembered another answer. Do you want to hear it?

Sal: Sure. I'm always in the market for that.

Chris: It's the three greatest values in the world.

Sal: Faith, hope, and love?

Chris: Yes.

Sal: How do they answer my question? How are they prayers?

Chris: There's the prayer of faith, the prayer of hope, and the prayer of love.

Sal: What's the prayer of faith?   *Prayer of faith*

Chris: There are two ways to pray it, with or without formulas.

Sal: Which is better?

Chris: Wrong question. We need both.

Sal: Why?

Chris: Well, if we can't just tell God what we believe in our own words sometimes, then there's something wrong. It's like your teachers' favorite kind of test question: "Explain in your own words . . ." If you can do that, it proves you understand the point, not just the words, because you can translate the point from someone else's words into your own. If you can't do that, then all you did is memorize the words, not understand the point.

Why we use formulas **Sal:** I see. And why do we need the other kind, the formulas?

Chris: Because they enlarge us. The words are greater than our own. Using them is like wearing great robes or living in a castle.

Sal: What great words?

Chris: The great, precious prayers the Church has cherished and used and preserved and handed down through the centuries like treasures. The prayers of faith are the creeds, and the best one for prayer is the first and oldest one of all, which is also the shortest and simplest: the Apostles' Creed. You know it, of course?

Sal: Yes. But I didn't realize it was a prayer.

Chris: It can be. And when you speak those great words, words as great as worlds, dripping with history, the whole Church prays with you, just as when you recite the Pledge of Allegiance to the flag, the whole country is with you.

Sal: I didn't realize that you can pray creeds. What else can you pray?

Chris: If anything *can't* be prayed, it shouldn't be spoken at all. There's a touchstone for all words. Deeds too, for that matter.

Sal: What do you mean by that?

Chris: I mean that in prayer you stand before God; you unveil yourself; you stand in the Presence, the Light, the Truth. Anything false or evil is afraid of that light and makes you ashamed to step into it. So whatever you can say or do as a prayer in the presence of God is good, and whatever you can't, is evil.

Sal: That sounds like a terribly practical guide to living and decision making.   *A guide to living*

Chris: It is! And that makes the point of our first long conversation even more important.

Sal: What point was that?

Chris: The one about just doing it, not running away from prayer with excuses like "no time". When we want to say something bad, we can't pray. You just couldn't put cruel words or gossip or blasphemy into a prayer, unless your conscience were dead. So when we want to say things like that, we run away from prayer. It's exactly those times when we most need to pray: times when we least want to.

Sal: The same thing works for deeds as for words, doesn't it?

Chris: Yes. What we can't do in God's presence, we shouldn't do at all. What we can't offer to God shouldn't stay. It's garbage.

Sal: That's certainly not a comfortable thing to admit. There's a lot of garbage in our lives, then.

Chris: But it's true, isn't it?

Sal: Yes.

Chris: Then we need to admit it. Truth is our food. We grow only by truth, as a plant grows only with water and sunlight.

Sal: And what about the prayer of hope? Hope can be a prayer too, right?   *Prayer of hope*

Chris: Right.

Sal: Are there two kinds of that too, informal and formal? Are there formulas for hope?

Chris: Mainly, they're part of the creeds: "the resurrection of the body and the life everlasting". But you can expand the prayer of hope, you can festoon those words.

Sal: How?

Chris: One way is to pick out all the promises God gave us in his word.

Sal: Promises?

Chris: Yes. The object of hope is God's promises.

Sal: Hope isn't just a thing inside of us, then.

Chris: No. It's a response to God's initiative. Like faith: it's not our feeling bottled up inside us, but our acceptance of what God has given us. It's specific, not vague. We don't just "believe" or just "hope"; we believe what God has told us, and we hope for what God has promised us.

Sal: I see. How do you pick out the promises in Scripture?

Promises in Scripture

Chris: You could just turn to some well known passage that you remember that has promises in it, like Isaiah 43, or John 14. Or you could just consult your memory. Or you could make a list. There are hundreds of promises in the Bible, especially in the words of Jesus.

Sal: And what do we do with them once we list them or remember them?

Chris: Confess them, express to God our belief in them.

Sal: Belief? I thought that was faith.

Chris: Hope *is* faith, directed to the future.

Sal: I see. So we can confess our hope just as we confess our faith.

Chris: Yes. But remember, it's prayer; it's between you and God; it's to him; it's dialogue.

Sal: Can you be more specific about what difference that makes?

Chris: It means we *claim* God's promises; we hold him to his word.

Sal: Oh! Isn't that . . . sort of presumptuous? Arrogant?

Chris: If I promise you something great, is it arrogant for you to expect me to come through? Isn't it arrogant *not* to? How dare we say this to God?—"I know you promised me wonderful things, things 'eye has not seen, ear has not heard, nor has it entered into the heart of man, the things God has prepared for those who love him.' I know you promised things like 'whatever you ask for in my name, I will give you', and 'all things work together for good for those who love God.' But I won't claim that. I won't expect you to give me what you promised me." Isn't *that* arrogant?

Sal: I guess so. So God wants us to be bold in claiming some of his promises?

Chris: No, *all* of them. But, remember, in his time and his way. He already pinned himself down to delivering a tremendous load of promises, but you can't pin him down any more than he pinned himself down. He might surprise you with his delivery schedule or with his delivery vehicle. His time and his way. But he'll deliver, or else he's not God.

Sal: That's indisputable. All right, let's talk about the prayer of love now. We talked about that already a bit, when we talked about adoration, right?

Prayer of love

Chris: Yes. It's not just any kind of love, but *agape*, the kind of love God has, unselfish love.

Sal: That's hard to put into words sometimes.

Chris: Yes, because it's so simple.

Sal: There are two forms for that prayer, too, I suppose? Formulas and no formulas?

Chris: Yes. And silence, a third way. Instead of *telling* God you love him, you just sit there and love him.

Sal: I understand that. And I understand how you also want to use words. Lovers do both. But I don't understand how love would want to use formulas.

Chris: The magic word is a formula, for one thing.

Sal: The magic word?

Chris: Yes: "I love you." That works magic, doesn't it?

Sal: Yes, and I understand how we can just say, "I love you, Jesus, I love you, Jesus", again and again. But what else?

Chris: We could say the *three* magic words.

Sal: What's that?

Chris: "Jesus, I love you. Thank you for loving me. Please help me to love you more."

Sal: Hmmm . . . I guess that says it all. I see. When you said our prayers could be like love songs, I thought you meant something longer.

Chris: They can be that too. Many of the great hymns of the Church are love prayers. Like the ones from Saint Bernard of Clairvaux.

Saint Bernard's ladder of love *Sal:* Oh, yes. He was a great theologian of love, wasn't he?

Chris: Yes. He explained the four rungs on the ladder of learning love. Do you know that?

Sal: No. Tell me.

Chris: First, we naturally love ourselves for our own sake—natural selfishness. Then, we learn to love *God* above all, but still for our own sake, for what God can do for us. Third, we learn to love God for God's sake. We forget ourselves in adoration. Then the fourth step is loving ourselves for God's sake. If God loves us, we should love ourselves for the love of God, just as we love our neighbors for the love of God. So if we go through steps two and three, we can change step one into step four; if we go through God-love, we can change selfish self-love into unselfish self-love.

Sal: That's beautiful.

Chris: And also true.

Loving your neighbor *Sal:* But it's only about loving God and self. What about loving your neighbor, loving other people? I know that's essential, but can that be a prayer too? If it could, it would bring together the traditional Christians, who seem to emphasize prayer, and the modern Christians, who emphasize helping and loving your neighbor.

Chris: Yes. There's no need for these two emphases to exclude each other. Loving your neighbors and working for them can be a prayer, and prayer can be a way to work for your neighbors.

Sal: How can each of those two things be the other? How does that work?

Chris: First, loving your neighbor can be prayer because it's loving Christ in your neighbor. You know Jesus' saying, "Inasmuch as you did it to one of the least of these my brothers, you did it to me." That works for good deeds *and* bad deeds. And second, prayer can be loving your neighbor when it's intercessory prayer. We didn't talk about that much: making a prayer list, becoming a prayer warrior, saving the world through prayer.

Sal: That would do a lot to heal the divisions between conservatives and liberals, wouldn't it? The favorite emphasis of each camp turns out to be done best by what the other camp emphasizes!

Chris: Yes, if conservatives would work as hard as liberals and liberals would pray as hard as conservatives, we'd win the world. All the great saints do both. Look at Mother Teresa, for instance. Is there any conflict, any gap, even, between her prayer and her work?

Sal: No, they fit together perfectly.

Chris: More than that. They're the same thing: God's own life in her, through her, God acting by means of her. "Grace" is another word for it. It's God's gift of himself. The gift comes into us by prayer and faith and comes out of us by works and love. It's like flowing water. It's the same water, the same reality, whether

Everything is grace.

in the form of faith or works, prayer or love. It's the same divine fire, first caught by faith, then passed on by love and the works of love. Faith without works is dead—like the Dead Sea, receiving fresh water but not passing it on. And works without faith are like trying to irrigate a desert from your swimming pool. You have to be open at both ends. You receive God by faith and pass him on by works of love. That keeps it fresh.

Sal: Loving God and loving neighbor are really one thing too? Vertical love and horizontal love? It's that same fire, isn't it?

Chris: Yes. Loving God in prayer and neighbor in work, loving God supernaturally and neighbor naturally, loving God in contemplation and neighbor in action—these are not two things, two realities, but one reality in two directions. Like sunlight reflected in two mirrors set at different angles. It's the same light, from the same sun.

Sal: That's it, isn't it? I mean, that double love is all you need, isn't it? So the song is right, "Love is all you need."

Chris: Yes, but it has to be true love, so you need truth too. And faith in God's Word is the way to truth for us, so you need faith too, and God's Word. And God's love is supernatural, above our natural powers, so we need grace, we need God to give it as a gift. And that comes only through Christ, so we need Christ. And the Church tells us about Christ, so we need the Church. You see, it's true to say love is all you need, but you have to remember two things about that truth: first, that it's God's love, not just fallen, finite, fallible human love that we need; and secondly that to get it we need all those other things God has provided for us too: truth and faith and grace and Christ and Church and Scripture.

Sal: But love is the greatest thing. So the prayer of love is the greatest prayer.

Chris: Yes. And we'll do it in heaven forever without ever being bored. So we'd better get some practice in here.

Sal: Instead of just talking about it again.

Chris: The talk is good, if it leads us to do it. It's bad only if it's an excuse for not doing it.

Sal: But how? Any specific suggestions for action?

Chris: I'm glad you asked. I almost forgot to mention something that answers that question, something Scripture very often links to prayer. I mean fasting.

Sal: Let's talk about fasting some other time, if you want; I want an answer about prayer right now: How do I practice the *prayer* of love?

Chris: But fasting *is* a form of prayer, not a separate thing. It *can* be a separate thing: for dieting, for self-discipline, or for freeing yourself from addiction to food, therapy for gluttony. But it can also be a means of prayer, a form of prayer.

Sal: A form of prayer of love?

Chris: Yes, and of other prayers too. We can fast simply to adore God, to worship, to say "Thy will, not mine, be done." Or we can fast in thanksgiving, we give God a gift as a way of saying "Thanks." Or we can fast in reparation for sin, in penance . . .

Sal: To take away sin? Didn't Christ do that?

Chris: Yes, and we don't do it to make up for any deficiencies in what he did, but to join ourselves to what he did. He did it completely, but that doesn't mean we can't do it with him. But the purpose of fasting that you're interested in now is love—fasting as the prayer of love, right?

Sal: Right.

Chris: That would be fasting for intercession, for others, giving up something for others.

Sal: How does that work? How does my going without something help somebody else?

Chris: I'm not sure *how* it works. But I know *that* it works, just because God told us.

Sal: In the Bible, you mean?

Chris: Yes. For instance, when Jesus' disciples tried to cast out a demon and couldn't, Jesus said, "This kind can be cast out only by prayer and fasting." It really works. God wouldn't have told us to do it if it didn't.

Sal: Can we give up other things besides food for others? Will that work too as a prayer?

Chris: Oh, yes. Sacrifices. There are hundreds of opportunities every day to give up innocent little things —good things, not just bad things—and that's a way of praying, a way of doing something *for* others. It's especially good for people who don't have a lot of thoughts and feelings and experiences in prayer, but want to do something practical, something active. It's a way of becoming freed from dependence on feelings, freed from the focus on experience. You *just do it*, that's all, and that's a real prayer. And I know it works; I've seen it work in my own life.

Sal: Wow!

Chris: But it's not magic, not button-pushing. We can't compel God by it.

Sal: Oh, I know that.

Chris: And we have to be reasonable about it. Don't starve yourself into sickness, or weakness, or flog yourself with a whip.

Sal: I don't think many people are in danger of doing that today.

Chris: No, but a few might be, and we should caution them.

Sal: Thanks for all the practical advice, Chris. Now's the time to try it, I think.

Chris: Not *try* it—that's the attitude of the scientist, the experimenter. No, *do* it, in faith. "Try it" means it might not be true. "Do it" means it is true, and you do it because it's true, it's real.

Dialogue Eight

The Prayers God Wrote for Us

Sal: Chris, you said the other day that when Jesus' disciples asked him, "Teach us to pray", he didn't give them a technique but a prayer, the Lord's Prayer. Doesn't that mean that's our answer too? We're his disciples too, after all.

Chris: Yes, we are. And yes, that is our answer. But that doesn't mean it's our *only* answer, just our number one answer. That's the perfect prayer, the model prayer. It doesn't mean we shouldn't use techniques, any more than it means we shouldn't use any other prayers. Anything that helps us get closer to him is good, and anything that doesn't, isn't. Techniques can be very helpful to many people, and we'll have a look at some of them soon. But they're only ours, not God's. They're not commanded in our Scriptures, as they are in Hindu and Buddhist scriptures. But neither are they forbidden. So before we talk about techniques, we should talk about the Lord's Prayer and other prayers God gave us in his Word.

Sal: O.K. There are a lot of prayers scattered throughout the Bible, aren't there?

Chris: Yes, and we can copy some of them down and put them in a little book to make them our own and

The Bible can be prayer.

101

remember them, especially the ones said to Jesus, like "Lord, I believe, help thou my unbelief", or "Lord, I am not worthy that you should come under my roof", or "Lord, teach us to pray." But the whole Bible can be a prayer too.

Sal: I didn't know that. How can the whole Bible be a prayer?

Chris: Oh, that's a precious thing. No Christian should miss that. It's the best way to read the Bible: as prayer. You can combine prayer and Bible reading, not just do both separately.

Sal: I knew there were prayers in the Bible, but I didn't know the Bible could be in prayer. I mean, I thought one form of literature in the Bible was prayer, but you're saying that one form of prayer is reading the Bible, right?

Chris: Yes. Both are true. Each contains the other. And each can bring the other home to us, strengthen the other. On the one hand, the prayers in the Bible are the best prayers, because they're part of God's revelation, they're prayers God arranged for us to have, especially the Lord's Prayer, so that we can pray them in confidence that God wants us to use them. Prayers we make up ourselves may be very good and very true and very beautiful too, but we can never have the confidence that God wrote them for us, or inspired them, as he inspired the Bible. On the other hand, reading the Bible *in* prayer, *as* a prayer—that lights up the Bible, that gives God a chance to show us deeper meanings in his Word. It's like reading a letter in the presence of the author. He's there to interpret the words to you. "God is his own interpreter", as the old hymn says. So reading the words as prayer, with the author present, is much better than reading the words just as words, as a substitute for the author.

Sal: That certainly makes a lot of sense. So reading

Scripture as a form of prayer means reading it in God's presence?

Chris: Yes.

Sal: But God is always present, isn't he?

Chris: Yes, but we don't always "practice the presence", open ourselves to it, to him. We should talk sometime about practicing the presence of God all day, in the middle of our daily work. For now, just remember the man in the picture.

Sal: You mean the puzzle picture you talked about the other day?

Chris: Yes. Every word in the Bible is like a stroke of the brush that paints God's portrait for us.

Sal: So when we read the words, we're really looking at a picture.

Chris: Even more than that, we're not just staring at a picture, we're actually meeting the Person. He's there! *Here.*

Sal: Even when he doesn't seem to be? Like in the Book of Job, when Job was searching for him for so long?

Chris: Yes. And Job's faith kept reaching out to him, even in the darkness.

Reaching out to God

Sal: That sounds beautiful, but what, exactly, does it mean, concretely, specifically, practically?

Chris: It means that Job kept praying, kept talking to God. His three friends only talked *about* God, as if he were absent. That's why God answered Job, but not the three friends, and why he said Job had spoken rightly, but not the three friends. Not all of Job's words or thoughts were correct, but he spoke rightly because he spoke to God, the God who was there.

Sal: And that's why God answered?

Chris: Yes. If we talk to God, he'll always answer us too, in one way or another. The Psalms are constantly promising that. The refrain is repeated many times: "I cried unto the Lord, and he answered me."

Sal: How? How does God answer?

Chris: In many ways. One way is in the very reading of the Bible itself. It's his Word, after all. Reading the Bible can be a two-way conversation, not just one-way.

Sal: You said when we were talking about the Holy Spirit that the Spirit uses Scripture as a sword—is that what makes it come alive and talk back to you?

Chris: Yes.

Praying for texts   *Sal:* What about opening the Bible at random to find an answer? I read about some holy person who did that, and he got just the answer he needed.

Chris: God never promised he'd do that for everybody. Sometimes he answers that way, but I don't think we should presume that he'll do it. That would make it mechanical, and manipulative, and magical—sort of like using God as a fortune-telling machine. No, when he performs any kind of miracle, it's from his initiative, not ours. He hasn't promised to give us the right texts every time we randomly flip through the Bible. But he *has* promised to lead us into the truth by his Word. David said, "Thy word is a lamp unto my feet and a light unto my path." Jesus said, "Thy Word is Truth", as he was praying to his Father for guidance for his disciples, for us. It's in John 17: "Father, lead them into the Truth; thy Word is Truth."

Sal: How does he do that, then, if it's not by flipping to a random text?

Chris: I don't know how *he* does it from his end. But from our end, I know some of the things we should do.

How to read Scripture   *Sal:* That's what I mean. What should I do so that the Bible lights up for me and comes alive as the Sword of the Spirit?

Chris: You've already done the first and most important thing: you want it. "Seek and you shall find"; he promised us that.

Sal: That's reassuring to know. Now *how* should I seek?

Chris: That's the next question, yes. I think, above all, you should pray, before, during, and after reading Scripture. Before we read, we should ask God to speak to us whatever he wants us to hear, as Samuel did in the Old Testament story. Samuel heard God calling him, and asked old Eli what to do. Eli told him to pray, "Speak, Lord, your servant is listening." We should put our mind at God's disposal. And even more important, our will. If we pray *and mean* "Thy will be done", before we read, that lets God do his will to us.

Sal: Lets him? Can we stop him?

Chris: We can't change him; the light always shines from him. But we can block it from getting in. He respects our freedom. He waits until he's invited in.

Sal: The prayer before reading can be very short and simple, then.

Chris: Yes. But not a hurried formula, not mere words. The more we mean it, the more God will act. Really let him lead you. Take the time to tame and quiet your desires, which are running off in a thousand different directions most of the time, and for a minute or two desire one thing and one thing only: God's will. Once you give God your will, even if you still have a thousand different desires and worries running around making it hard to be still, God will take you at your word, and you'll begin to see things happen as you read, and afterward too.

Sal: That "Thy will be done" prayer is good for anything, isn't it, not just reading Scripture?

Chris: It sure is.

Sal: You said we should pray before, during, and after. I think I understand the "before"—laying down our will and mind to God. And the "during"—practicing his presence, seeing the Man in the picture, the lover behind the love letter. What's the "after"?

Chris: Wait a minute. There's more to the "during" first.

Sal: Oh, oh.

Chris: What's the matter? Don't you want more help?

Sal: Of course. I just don't want it to be too complex.

There are many techniques. *Chris:* It isn't. It's all quite simple. All that I can tell you is a few elementary things, remember—much less than many books on prayer tell you. They make it look complex sometimes, especially if they talk a lot about techniques. But even if I gave you a hundred different techniques, that's not something to say "Oh, oh" about, because it's not an obligation. You don't have to do any of them. Whatever works for you, that's all. You freely choose whatever kinds of prayer you want to use.

Sal: What? You mean religion is like a supermarket? You just come in and pick whatever you like and leave the rest?

Chris: No, not in doctrines. We believe *everything* God revealed. And not in morality: we do *everything* God commanded, or try to. But in kinds of prayer, yes. Different kinds work for different people; that's why there are so many different kinds. God never commanded just one kind of prayer for everyone.

Sal: Just the Lord's Prayer.

Chris: That's not a *kind* of prayer; that's a prayer.

Sal: O.K., so I won't feel threatened by the many different kinds of prayer and techniques of prayer, even if you tell me many of them. I don't have to do them all. I guess I'll try them all and then stay with the ones that seem to work.

Chris: Fine. But what do you mean by "the ones that seem to *work*"?

Sal: The ones that seem to bring me and God together. The ones that I believe God wants for me.

Chris: Good. Yes, those are the ones you should use.

Sal: O.K., now what else were you going to tell me about praying while reading Scripture?

Chris: To read very slowly. Sink into the words. Ruminate, like a cow chewing her cud. Don't be impatient to cover a certain number of verses. Just explore the meanings of a very few, slowly and meditatively. Poke around. Enjoy. Don't push it, don't force it.

Read Scripture slowly.

Sal: O.K., that slows me down. What do I look for in the verses?

Chris: Not what a scholar would look for. Don't *study* it as if you're going to take a test on it, or write an article about it. Don't analyze it. It's not a puzzle. It's an ocean. You swim in it.

Sal: Is that hard or easy to do?

Chris: It can be hard, at first, if you're not in the habit of slowing down. Your mind is probably like a fast car, and you need to apply the brakes. But once you do, you sort of glide in neutral downhill, letting the gravity of the verse itself move you, instead of pushing the car with your motor going hot and heavy. It's like sailing instead of motorboating, or gliding instead of flying a plane with a motor. You just slow down and let the verse itself move you, let the Spirit move you along as the wind moves a sailboat along the water.

Sal: Sounds lazy. I'm afraid I'd fall asleep.

Chris: No, it's the opposite of lazy; it's waking up. Try it somewhere else first: try slowing down outside and taking fifteen minutes to do nothing at all but listen to all the sounds you hear, or look at blades of grass, or trees, or clouds, or feel every part of your body one by one. *Notice* things, instead of just *seeing* them. We see a lot, but we notice only a little most of the time. We rush past things so fast.

Sal: I'm afraid I'd get bored very quickly just look-ing at grass for fifteen minutes—or just one verse of Scripture for fifteen minutes.

Chris: I don't think you will. I think it will be tremen-dously exciting for you.

Sal: Why?

Discovering things in Scripture *Chris:* Because you'll have the thrill of new discovery. You'll notice and appreciate dimensions you never did before.

Sal: What if nothing comes to mind as I think about my verse?

Chris: Then go on to the next one. But give it a chance first. Quite often God wants to tell us something, either through his Word or through his world, and we just don't hear him because we're rushing around too fast and making too much of our own noise. He says, "Be still and know that I am God", and we reply, "No, I want to keep moving and making noises." Our whole modern age and world and mind glorifies speed and movement, not rest and silence. So it's hard for us to hear God, because he speaks "with a still, small voice" from the silence, not with a shout from the hubbub of a thousand other shouts that drown him out. It's just not his style to out-shout us; he waits until we're quiet, until we're listening, until we *want* to hear him. He's quite a gentleman.

Sal: This prayer of quiet—that's contemplative prayer, isn't it?

Chris: As an attitude of mind for reading Scripture, it's sort of halfway to it.

Sal: I don't understand.

Chris: We should talk about pure contemplative prayer later. But that is so foreign to our activistic modern mind that most people need an intermediate form of prayer, where they're not *totally* silent and empty, just slowed down a bit and listening, but where there's something to do, some external aids, like crutches.

Sal: What are those?

Chris: The words of Scripture.

Sal: I see. So we can learn more and more of contemplative prayer by learning to read Scripture more contemplatively.

Chris: Yes.

Sal: All right. Now what about the "after"? How do we pray after reading Scripture?

Chris: Jesus said his words should "abide" in us, *dwell* in us, live in us, as you dwell in a dwelling, a house, or "abide" in a country: you live there all the time, even when you're not consciously thinking about it. It's habitual, second nature. We can usually put only a few minutes of our time into reading God's Word, but we can put God's Word into all of our time. We can carry the Bible around in our minds and hearts, as we would carry a love letter: we remember it, it makes a difference to us, it makes us what we are.

Abiding in God's Word

Sal: That's the "after"?

Chris: Yes.

Sal: And does this happen by itself if we've done the rest? Or is there some technique for the "after"?

Chris: It happens by itself. But we can aid the process by remembering Scripture.

Sal: Conscious memorizing?

Memorization

Chris: That's a good way, yes, but not the only way.

Sal: Isn't memorization old-fashioned?

Chris: So? Should we throw it out just because it's old-fashioned? Honesty and courage and loyalty and chastity are old-fashioned too. So are our grandparents! Should we throw them out?

Sal: Of course not. I just meant that memorization isn't enough. Understanding is more important.

Chris: Of course it's not enough. And if some older teachers thought it was, that was a serious educational mistake. But it helps. When you need something more than a vague, wordless feeling to draw on, it's a great help to have a storehouse of memorized texts to use. It's practical—like weapons, or tools. We carry them around in our mental toolbox, our memory, to bring out and use when we need them.

Sal: I see. But how do we learn them? Most teachers don't make us memorize them anymore. And we don't have a lot of time to spend just consciously memorizing and testing ourselves.

Chris: You could just pick out one verse a day, or even part of a verse—perhaps something from the bit of Scripture that you read or prayed that day— and repeat it frequently during the day, each time you remember to do it. That way, you get two benefits: you carry God's own words into your life, into your day, to light up your day, and you also remember the verse by repeating it so much.

Sal: Must the verse be a prayer?

Chris: Not necessarily. It can. But you can illuminate the day with any great verse. For instance, "In the beginning God created the heavens and the earth." As you go through the day, through the world, you remind yourself that this whole world came straight from God's hands, that he owns all of it and loves all of it. It gives you a different perspective on everything. Or a verse like "Feed my sheep." We're supposed to help others because they're Jesus' sheep, his precious ones. Or "Behold I am with you always." There are thousands of verses that are like little matches, ready to light your whole day on fire and spread the fire through your life.

Sal: That's what I need: practical things to do like that. Are there any other ways you know to make Scripture come alive like that?

Chris: Well, of course, the basic thing is not any method or gimmick, but *desire*. If you want it truly and passionately, God will give it. If you ask him for his promise, he'll give it to you. And his promise here is the Holy Spirit. *He* makes Scripture come alive, not our little gimmicks. But we can use our little gimmicks as doors that we open to him, ways of inviting him in.

Sal: Now that I know the right perspective on them, do you know any more gimmicks?

Chris: One good one for many people is fantasy. For some reason, most people seldom use their imagination in prayer, only their mind and will. But Jesus appealed to the imagination with his parables and images and symbols. So we're invited to use this God-given faculty too.

Using imagination

Sal: How?

Chris: Imagine you're *in* the stories you read in Scripture. Let yourself go. Forget you're sitting in a chair in the twentieth century. Imagine you're walking the dusty roads of Palestine with Jesus. Take time to imagine details. Put in details of your own to go with the few details you find in Scripture. Imagine how you'd feel if you were there. Imagine yourself talking with Jesus—imagine him talking to you.

Sal: Daydream, eh?

Chris: Yes. Some people just can't do it, but most can. Some can do it best by just letting themselves go, without consciously or deliberately trying. Others find it works better when they systematically control it step by step, detail by detail. Try it; see what works for you. If you've never done anything like that before, give it quite a few tries before you give up on it; the imagination is like a muscle: it has to be used a little to become strong, but with exercise it can improve a lot.

Sal: That sounds exciting. We can travel through time and space that way, we can go right back to Jesus' time and place. Any other methods?

Writing letters to God

Chris: Many people find writing letters to God a good way of praying, and you can combine that with reading Scripture by imagining Scripture as letters from God. You write letters back to him about his letters to you, and also about your life and feelings and needs, and then look for his answers. But don't expect to find them without looking. For instance, if you tell him you're lonely, find the passages in the Bible where it talks about being alone and not being alone. Use a study Bible, with topics and subtopics and indexes. Don't expect to find answers just by flipping open the Bible and expecting a miracle each time.

Sal: Sometimes I can say more in writing than in talking. That makes sense, to write letters to God. I can write my own personal, private prayers.

Chris: Yes. You take them more seriously when they're written down. It gives them a permanence. Spoken words go by so quickly.

Sal: Do you think we can keep up a long dialogue like that, God and I, by letter?

Chris: By everything. What is life but a relationship with God, a dialogue with God? So this exercise is very realistic, very true to life.

Sal: It's not arrogant to talk back to God, to question him?

Chris: Certainly not. God doesn't want vegetables. He wants you to come to him with all your needs, including questions and uncertainties and ignorance and doubts. Even a merely human book can come alive for you once you dialogue with it, ask questions of it, look for answers in it. How much more the book that's the Sword of the Spirit?

Sal: I think those are enough methods and exercises for me. I don't want to get confused. What do we look at next?

Chris: You're right to want to keep it simple. Better keep at just a few methods, than keep toying with all of them. Let's look at a book of prayers God wrote for us next. Inspired men to write, I mean.

Sal: You mean the Psalms?

The Psalms

Chris: Yes. You can find some good books on the Psalms and how to pray them, from people like C. S. Lewis and Thomas Merton. And there are many books of meditations on the different Psalms. So all I'll give you is a few general pieces of practical advice.

Sal: O.K.

Chris: For one thing, they're songs. We can literally sing them if we like, improvising a tune or using a chant or anything we like, anything we can find or make.

Sal: I'm a terrible singer.

Chris: Do you think God minds? He isn't marking you, you know. The Psalm doesn't tell us to make a professional performance unto the Lord, just to "make a joyful noise unto the Lord".

Sal: I can do that, all right. But I still think it would feel funny.

Chris: Then just recite the Psalms as poems. Some people find singing helps, but not everybody. There are many ways to praise. Some people find *listening* to great music a way of praying. Some people love to chant, like most cultures in the past. There are chant forms for the Psalms, or you can just improvise your own.

Sal: That would have to be *very* private! If anybody heard me improvising chants, they'd think I flipped.

Chris: The important thing is not what you do with your body and your mouth when you pray the Psalms, but what you do with your soul.

Sal: You mean bodily acts and sounds aren't important?

Chris: No, I don't mean that. I mean you should use whatever feels right for you, whatever works best to put your soul nearer God. Whatever helps you pray them with your whole soul.

Sal: My whole soul?

Chris: Yes: not just the conscious mind, but the unconscious and the imagination and memory and association and the will and feeling and contemplation, as well as reason.

Sal: Sounds pretty spontaneous inside, even though there are set words outside.

Chris: That's right. The Psalms aren't like long-playing records that we just passively listen to on a record player, that sound the same every time no matter who plays them, but they are like a piece of sheet music that you have to interpret on your instrument. And they sound different each time and with each different person who uses them. Because you put your individual self into them, they're more like frames, and you paint the picture.

Sal: I see. The Lord's Prayer is like that too, isn't it?

Chris: Yes, even more so.

Praying the Psalms spontaneously

Sal: So we can be quite open and free and spontaneous when we pray the Psalms, even though the words are set.

Chris: Yes. The psalmists who composed them were totally open and honest before God, and the Psalms invite us to be the same. There's no need to fake anything, to work up a state in yourself that you think you ought to be in. Just tell God what you really think and feel, not what you think you ought to. The Psalms help you to do that.

Sal: So I should use the one that expresses how I feel?

Chris: Oh, yes.

Sal: I thought I should just go through them one by one, beginning with the first. *Where to start*

Chris: You *can*. But, to paraphrase a saying of Jesus, the Psalms were made for man, not man for the Psalms. They're for a variety of situations and moods.

Sal: I thought moods weren't important. Remember? Fact, then faith, then feeling.

Chris: They're not to be our objective or end. No mood is sacred. But even though they're not important for themselves, they're important as roads to be used to travel to God and for God to travel to us, so to speak. In fact, that's true of the whole world and everything in it: it's not our end, not sacred, but just a road, a means for God and us to meet, a *Between*. *Everything is a Between.*

Sal: I see. Then I think it would be practical for me to keep a list of my favorite Psalms and what moods they fit, so I can tell at a glance which one to use.

Chris: That's a practical idea. You can keep a list of favorites and gradually expand your list, using new Psalms and becoming familiar with them too, eventually.

Sal: I don't think I could use *all* of them. Don't some of them have cursings in them? Doesn't the writer say terrible things about his enemies?

Chris: Yes, in some of them. And Christians know better than that. But we can still use them, because we know who our real enemies are. Paul told us: "We wrestle not against flesh and blood but against principalities and powers . . . against spiritual forces of wickedness in heavenly places." Life *is* warfare, you know, spiritual warfare. We *do* have enemies, unless Jesus and the Bible are foolish. *The "cursing Psalms"*

116 / Prayer: The Great Conversation

Sal: Evil spirits, you mean? The Devil?

Chris: Yes.

Sal: I guess that must be true, because it's in the Bible. But it feels kind of primitive and superstitious.

Chris: Has any discovery of modern times proved they don't exist?

Sal: I guess not. But not many people believe in them anymore.

Chris: Is that how you decide what's true? By counting noses?

Sal: No. I'll go by one nose against a million if it's Jesus'. So there *is* the Devil and there are his fallen angels—whatever they are.

Evil spirits are the real enemy. *Chris:* It's true we don't know much about them. But we can use the cursing Psalms against them, because they're not human beings who might repent and whom we're commanded to love and pray for. If Adolf Hitler came to Jesus truly repentant, he'd forgive him. But Satan will never come and repent.

Sal: Let's talk about something less horrible.

Chris: Demons *are* horrible. But that doesn't mean we can ignore them completely. I think people in the past tended to make much too much of them, but I think people in the present make the opposite mistake: denying their very existence or ignoring them completely.

Sal: How do we know what's the right attitude and avoid falling into either extreme?

Chris: Whose attitude should be our model?

Sal: Jesus'. Of course. What a simple answer!

Chris: He's the answer God provided for *all* our needs. That's what the Bible says, anyway.

Sal: Why don't you hear many Christians admitting that, even from the pulpit?

Chris: I don't know. Maybe because we prefer to flatter our egos by saying a thousand clever things we make up, and it takes a big dose of humility and simple honesty to just preach and practice the one thing God gave us.

Sal: We've been wandering from our topic—and that's O.K. with me, because we've wandered into some pretty important things—but is there anything else I should know about the Psalms, do you think?

Chris: Much more, but not from me. Let's get to the Lord's Prayer. We've been narrowing our focus: first we talked about praying Scripture in general, then the Psalms, now this one prayer. I really can't tell you much about it, not because there's too little to say, but because there's too much. A whole world is there: the world of prayer. Many long books have been written about just those few words in the Lord's Prayer. I'm certainly not going to add one more, or preach a sermon to you, or interpret some of the meanings in each line. How about just one or two little pieces of practical advice?

The Lord's Prayer

Sal: Fine.

Chris: For one thing, it's not only a formal prayer, but also a guide to informal prayer, an outline of things for us to say to God. We should improvise on it, decorate it, festoon it, add variations to it, ring changes on it, dive off it, sow it as seeds, grow with it like a baby. It's a beginning, not an end. It's like an outline of a book; Jesus invites us to write our own book following his outline.

Sal: How should we do that?

Chris: Any way you like. But let me make one practical suggestion. Whenever you pray spontaneously and informally, whether you're improvising on the Lord's Prayer or not, I find it's better actually to open your mouth and say or whisper words—better than just thinking and feeling and keeping it in.

Sal: Why?

Chris: Because we get distracted so easily, and we daydream, or even fall asleep. The words help keep the mind clear. Words have a kind of feedback effect on the thoughts they express; expressing them in words makes the thoughts clearer and stronger. It's like training the nervous system to work better by training the muscles it controls. Usually the nerves move the muscles. But sometimes if there's damage to those nerves, you can help repair it by exercising the muscles. Then it works backward: the muscles move the nerves. That's how it is with thoughts and words: thoughts usually move the words, but words can help the thoughts to move better too. So I find—most people find, I think—that when they try to pray without words, they tend to get sloppy and sleepy. If so, just use words.

Sal: Aren't thoughts and feelings more important than words?

Chris: Yes, but it's silly to prefer vague thoughts and feelings to words that help the thoughts and feelings to become less vague.

Sal: But don't the great writers on prayer say wordless prayer is higher?

Chris: Wordless prayer, contemplative prayer, the prayer of silence, yes. But that's not *vague*. We'll talk about that some other time, O.K.?

Sal: O.K., but soon, I hope. O.K., what else about the Lord's Prayer?

Chris: Expect to discover things as you pray it. Even though it's very short, you find new truths in it all the time. It's like a cow that keeps giving you fresh milk every morning. After you've repeated those words a thousand times, you haven't begun to exhaust their meaning.

Sal: And I'll bet I should try to discover some of those

meanings with my heart, too, and not just my head, right?

Chris: You're getting to know me so well you can say it before I do!

Sal: Am I going too fast?

Chris: No, that's great. You're becoming your own teacher. That's what every good teacher wants to see.

Sal: But how do I discover things with my heart?

Chris: What you discover in a prayer isn't clever intellectual answers, or tricks, or hidden riddles, or brilliant new interpretations. No, it's more like a lover discovering in the same old beloved new joys every time they meet—yet they're the same old joys. Saint Augustine called God, "Beauty ever ancient and yet ever new." Think of two people married for fifty years, still deeply in love, not bored with each other, new every day, yet the same. Saint Paul calls Jesus "the same yesterday, today, and forever". Yet Jesus also says, "Behold, I make all things new." *Ever ancient, ever new*

Sal: And what you said before about prayer as two-way conversation, not just one-way—that's true here too, isn't it? This prayer is dialogue, not monologue, right?

Chris: Oh, yes. Expect answers. I have a friend, you know, who says that when he prays, "Thy kingdom come", he looks around to see what's coming.

Sal: That's a good one!

Chris: No, that's a *right* one. God told us to ask for it; don't you think he'll give us what he commanded us to ask for?

Sal: I do. I know prayer isn't talking to yourself.

Chris: And you know that the One you talk to isn't asleep. He's so awake and active that he created the whole universe! And he never changes, so he's just as active now.

Sal: Like pure energy, yet a Person. That's awesome!

Chris: Even more awesome, he lets us touch him by prayer.

Sal: I think we'd better plug into that dynamo instead of just talking about it all day.

Chris: Now you're really learning!

Dialogue Nine

How to Shut up and Let God Show Up

Sal: Chris, I could hardly wait for today.

Chris: Why?

Sal: Because today's the day you promised to talk about contemplation, or meditation, or the Prayer of Silence.

Chris: And why are you so impatient to talk about that?

Sal: Because it seems to be the highest of all kinds of prayer. *The highest form of prayer*

Chris: Why do you think it's the highest?

Sal: Because it's the most intimate with God. And because the great saints and mystics say so. I've read a little bit of their writings, and it seems overwhelmingly attractive, just beautiful, wonderful, the greatest thing in the world, a foretaste of Heaven on earth.

Chris: And do you expect to have a foretaste of heaven on earth?

Sal: *Expect* it? No. I know it's a free gift, not something I can demand by right or produce by force.

Chris: Good for you.

Sal: But I aspire to it. I hope for it. Is that wrong?

Chris: No, no, a thousand times no. What better goal could anyone ever have in this life? But I think I should give you two warnings.

Sal: Go ahead.

Chris: First, be sure you're looking for God, not for experiences.

Sal: I know. The great writers call them "sensible consolations", right?

Chris: Yes. And they're very tempting, because they give the very highest joy anyone can possibly ever experience on earth.

Sal: Why do you call that a temptation? If the joy comes from God, it's good, isn't it?

Chris: Very good. But it just won't come if you look for it. It's like human happiness: if you worry about it and keep turning inward to see whether you're happy or not, you'll never be happy. You can be happy only when you forget yourself and lose yourself in something you love. So with this higher happiness: it comes only when you forget about it, never when you aim at it.

Sal: I understand. That's why we have to aim at God, not it.

Chris: We *do* have to aim at God, not it; but the reason for that isn't just because it *works* if we do that, but because God deserves our adoration, because we shouldn't seek anything above God, not even the joys God can give. The Giver should come first, not the gifts —and we should put him first, not just as a gimmick for getting the gifts, either, but for his own sake.

Sal: I understand.

Chris: God spices himself up sometimes, but he doesn't want us to get a spiritual sweet tooth and seek only the spices instead of the food, only the joys God sometimes clothes himself in instead of the Person behind the clothes. It's the same God who comes to

Sensible consolations

us unspiced most of the time, unclothed in joys, or "sensible consolations", like Santa Claus without any presents. That was the test he gave Job: do you still love *me* when all my gifts are gone?

Sal: So the joy comes only when we don't seek it.

Chris: Yes, because joy is only God's perfume. It's a sign, a clue. It points to God. But if we stand there and sniff the sign instead of following it, we'll never get anywhere.

Sal: I understand. What's the second warning?

Chris: Patience. You have to learn to crawl before you can walk and to walk before you can run.

Sal: I know that. But all the saints say contemplation is for everyone, not just for the elite. Isn't that true?

Contemplation is for everyone.

Chris: Yes, it's true.

Sal: Then it's even for me.

Chris: Yes, it is. In God's time and God's way. It's a gift, remember.

Sal: Yes, but if I walk in the paths these others walked in, God will give those gifts to me too, won't he?

Chris: If you mean by that that you can expect to taste the riches they tasted merely by imitating their methods of prayer, no.

Sal: Oh, I know that—I know prayer isn't a mechanical thing. It's not like learning how to operate a machine, but like getting to know a person.

Chris: It's not *like* getting to know a person; it *is* getting to know a Person.

Sal: All right . . .

Chris: You must be sure of that!

Sal: I am. And I also know I'm only a beginner, so I should be patient. But even a tiny taste of the riches they describe would be more precious than the whole rest of the world, I think. Do you think I'm exaggerating?

Chris: Not at all. You're right, profoundly right. You see the beauty and the greatness of the mountain of prayer. Just be sure you remember where you are: only on a tiny foothill.

Sal: I like that image. It's not only humbling, but hopeful too. Because it's the same mountain, isn't it? The same God that both we and the greatest saints are climbing?

Chris: Yes. That's true.

Sal: I think of prayer as a ladder, with contemplative prayer as the topmost rung. Is that right?

Chris: Not if you mean you can leave the lower rungs behind when you climb to the higher rungs.

Sal: You mean the other kinds of prayer are just as exalted?

The basics are always necessary. *Chris:* Just as *important*. As your feet are just as important as your eyes. They hold you up. Even when you're on the higher rungs, you still need the lower rungs to hold you up. The simple basics of prayer are the necessary foundation for contemplative prayer. Contemplative prayer isn't that different from ordinary prayer, just purer and simpler and more complete. It's the same thing, after all: it's *prayer*.

Sal: But it's a different form of prayer, isn't it? Wordless and without concepts that can be put into words?

Chris: Yes.

Sal: Are contemplation and contemplative prayer and meditation and the Prayer of Silence all just about the same thing?

Chris: Just about. If there are distinctions, they're not as important for us as understanding the common essence of all these things you mentioned and, above all, how to do it.

Sal: Yes. That's what I want to know. Will you tell me now?

Chris: Didn't the great saints and mystics that you read tell you?

Sal: Yes . . .

Chris: Well, they're certainly much more qualified to teach it than I am, aren't they?

Sal: Yes.

Chris: Well then, why don't you follow their advice?

Sal: For one thing, it's difficult to understand sometimes.

Chris: Is that the main reason?

Sal: No.

Chris: What is it?

Sal: Well . . .

Chris: Why do you hesitate?

Sal: I had to make a deliberate decision to avoid dishonesty rather than embarrassment. The reason I don't follow their advice is basically that I'm lazy, and selfish, and sinful.

Obstacles to contemplation

Chris: Welcome to the human race!

Sal: But there's another thing: I'm not sure I *should.* I'm not sure contemplation is right for me.

Chris: What? I thought you longed for this. I thought you found it irresistibly attractive.

Sal: Oh, I do. But at the same time I feel a little guilty —no, not guilty, uncertain—uncertain whether this is what God wills for me or not.

Chris: Why do you feel that uncertainty? Don't the saints say it's for everybody?

Sal: Yes, but they're not infallible. So it's O.K. to question them, isn't it?

Chris: What's your question?

Sal: Contemplative prayer seems awfully passive.

Chris: Why? Because you don't do anything in it?

Sal: Yes.

Chris: You don't talk, for instance.

Sal: Yes.

Listening is active. *Chris:* Do you think talking is more active than listening?

Sal: Well . . . no, I guess it isn't. Not real listening. You need to be even more alert and aware and alive and awake to listen. You can go on talking automatically, without thinking, just quacking like a duck.

Chris: Right you are. So contemplation isn't passive. And here's another reason why contemplation is good: God himself commanded it.

Sal: Where?

Chris: "Be still and know that I am God."

Sal: Oh, yes. I forgot that.

Chris: And reason reinforces revelation here, too.

Sal: How?

Chris: Think: when you're talking with somebody less important than you, who does most of the talking?

Sal: I do.

Chris: And when you're talking with somebody equally important, you share the talking about equally, right?

Sal: Right.

Chris: And when you're talking with somebody more important than you—the wisest person in the world, say—who would you want to do most of the talking then?

We need to listen to God. *Sal:* The other person, of course. I'd want to listen all I could.

Chris: Well, all the more with God.

Sal: That makes sense. But here's another reason for my hesitation toward contemplative prayer. Jesus never taught it, did he?

Chris: Not in the Gospels, no.

Sal: And Jesus is our teacher, isn't he?

Chris: Yes.

Sal: The very best teacher, right?

Chris: Yes.

Sal: The complete teacher, then, right?

Chris: Yes, but to be a complete teacher is not to give the students all the complete answers, but to give them the basics, the tools, so they can educate themselves and find answers for themselves. Isn't that what a good teacher does? *Did Jesus teach everything?*

Sal: I guess so.

Chris: Jesus never taught science, or logic, or math, or history either. Does that mean we shouldn't?

Sal: Of course not. But that's not religion.

Chris: Jesus never defined the doctrine of the Trinity either, or gave any proofs for the existence of God, or created a systematic theology, or even wrote a Gospel. Does that mean the Church was wrong to make creeds to distinguish truth about the Trinity from falsehoods? Or that a philosopher like Saint Thomas Aquinas shouldn't have written five proofs for the existence of God? Or that all Christian teachers of systematic theology should be kicked out of theological schools? Or that Matthew, Mark, Luke, and John shouldn't have written their Gospels because Jesus never did?

Sal: No, no, of course not. I see your point. You can't argue that a thing is wrong just because Jesus didn't do it. But—look here, Chris, I've tried to be honest with you always, even if it was uncomfortable to me, because I know you never put me down, and I know you try to understand me. Well, I have this irrational little fear or something in me that makes me hesitate to try contemplative prayer, even though another part of me longs for it. I'm running to it and away from it at the same time, and I'm not sure why. I fear I'm idolizing it somehow.

Sanctity or mysticism?

Chris: Let's see whether you are. Suppose God offered you a choice between two gifts, two graces: sanctity or mystical prayer, contemplative prayer. You could be either a saint or a mystic, but not both. Which would you choose?

Sal: Let's define our terms first. What do you mean by a saint?

Chris: A holy person, one whose will and love are in line with God's will and love: one who loves God a lot, and loves what God loves, wills what God wills; one who obeys the two great commandments, to love God with all your heart and your neighbor as yourself.

Sal: And a mystic?

Chris: One who practices the heights of contemplative prayer, who tastes in prayer something of the joy and intimacy and understanding that we'll have in the "beatific vision" of God face to face in heaven.

Sal: Wow! That's quite a choice. Those two things are pretty closely connected, aren't they?

Chris: Yes, but which comes first?

Sal: I'd choose sanctity first, I think.

Chris: Good! Then you needn't feel guilty about desiring mystical contemplation, because you're not idolizing it, you're not putting it ahead of sanctity, you're not putting the second thing ahead of the first thing.

Sal: Why is sanctity greater than contemplation?

Chris: Because sanctity is loving God, and since God *is* love, it's the closest to God. That's why one writer said, "There is ultimately only one tragedy in life: not to have been a saint." There's the ultimate meaning of life in one sentence. Do you agree?

Sal: I agree.

Chris: Good. Then you're putting first things first. So you needn't feel hesitant about putting second things second instead of third or thirtieth.

Sal: And contemplation is a powerful friend and helper to sanctity and love, too, isn't it?

Chris: Oh, yes. That's why contemplation is such a great thing, and why the saints love it, and why you should, too.

Sal: O.K., my conscience is completely at rest. It's *not* an alternative to sanctity, but it can almost be an aspect of sanctity.

Chris: Or a means to it.

Sal: How does that work?

Contemplation is a means to sanctity.

Chris: In contemplative prayer, you're in God's presence. You don't want to sin then. Evil flees from that light almost as fast as the speed of light.

Sal: Almost as fast?

Chris: God's light always catches it.

Sal: I understand how contemplation is a means to sanctity. But isn't sanctity a means to contemplation too? Because if your heart is right with God, you can see him clearly, but if it isn't, you just don't understand him at all. In fact, you don't want to.

Chris: Absolutely right, Sal.

Sal: So which comes first? Contemplation or sanctity? The mind or the heart? Each one causes the other; each one comes first.

Chris: The heart comes first.

Sal: Prove it.

Chris: "Out of the heart are the issues of life"— that's in Proverbs. And in John 7:17, Jesus is talking to the Pharisees. They ask him how they can know his teaching, whether it comes from God or whether he's making it up on merely human authority. (A pretty important question, don't you think?) And Jesus answers, "If your will were to do the will of my Father, you would understand my teaching, that it comes from him." You see? If we love God, if our will is open to him, only then does our mind follow and do we understand him. The heart, the will, comes first.

Sal: So sanctity comes first.

Chris: Yes. Both in time and in value. Without sanctity, even contemplation is of no value, no value at all.

Sal: None at all?

Love of God comes first.

Chris: No. The greatest mystic in the world has only trash unless he loves God.

Sal: Can you prove that?

Chris: Sure. First Corinthians 13: "If I understand all mysteries and have not love, I am nothing."

Sal: That's pretty clear and unanswerable.

Chris: But contemplation is of tremendous value *with* sanctity. The two reinforce each other: the more we know God, the more we can love him, and the more we love him, the more we can know him—just as with each other. The more you know someone, the more you can love him, and the more you love him, the more deeply you come to know him.

Sal: I see. So contemplation should help us to overcome sin.

A remedy for sin

Chris: Yes, it should. Contemplation puts us into God's presence, and sin just can't live in that light. One of the most common mistakes Christians make in trying to overcome sin is ignoring this great remedy.

Sal: It's for ordinary Christians, then? For everybody?

Chris: Yes!

Sal: But mysticism is something special, something unusual.

Chris: You don't have to be a mystic to practice contemplative prayer. Simple, ordinary people are doing it right now, this very minute, all over the world.

Sal: Well, I'm certainly in the market for any remedy that might work against the world's worst disease.

Chris: And this works. New Year's resolutions don't. Trying a little harder doesn't. Agonized introspection and worry don't.

Sal: You're right there.

Chris: Do you know why they don't work?

Sal: Why?

Chris: Because they focus on yourself, not God. Contemplation looks at God. I'll bet the next time you're tempted to any sin, you won't want to pray, to look at God, right?

Sal: Well, not always. Sometimes I say, "God help me!" but he doesn't seem to help.

How to deal with temptation

Chris: Do you give him the time?

Sal: How?

Chris: Contemplation. Just stop whatever you're doing for a minute (that's the hardest step of all!) and look at God, realize you're in his presence.

Sal: When the temptation is immediate and concrete, God seems awfully abstract and remote.

Chris: Then contemplate Jesus, in all his humanity. Remember he's right there with you.

Sal: Talk to him?

Chris: Yes. But more important, let him talk to you. If you do that, you'll overcome any temptation in the world.

Sal: How do you know that?

Chris: Because for us to sin, we first have to look away from God. Sin can't live in his presence. Of course, don't expect instant success. It's hard to break our lifetime habits. Contemplation is a barrier against sin, but it's hard to get the barrier up. Even the great saints say that. Once it's up, it's effortless: God's the one who acts. But for us to *get* it up takes effort.

Sal: I understand that. But at least I see the value of contemplation now. It leads to sanctity, and anything that does that is good, right? And if anything leads to contemplation, it's good, too, right? Because contemplation in turn leads to sanctity.

Chris: What did you have in mind?

Oriental religions *Sal:* Techniques, especially the ones used by other religions, especially Eastern religions like Zen and TM —transcendental meditation. That comes from Hinduism, I'm told. I've wondered whether they're good means for a Christian to use as aids to contemplation.

Chris: I've wondered about that too. I think we should use Jesus' principle here: "by their fruits you shall know them." If they really lead you toward God, toward the true good and toward sanctity, they must be good. If not, not.

Sal: How might they lead you away from God?

Chris: If they make you think of God as Eastern religions do, as some cosmic, impersonal Force instead of the Person who revealed himself in the Bible, in Jesus. Oriental religions usually think of God that way, as a sort of cosmic consciousness instead of a Person you can love and trust and pray to. So you'd clearly have to separate out the meditation techniques from the theology.

Sal: Can you do that?

A possible use *Chris:* With some, I think. But not with the ones that
for Oriental induce any kind of trance, like the Hindu *samadhi*.
techniques Some say TM and Zen don't do that at all. So it sounds good in theory to use them. It sounds like it would be something like the medieval Christian theologians using Aristotle's logic after separating it out from Aristotle's philosophy. His logic was simply good logic, good for everyone, but his philosophy contradicted Christianity at a few points. Or maybe it's like a Christian psychiatrist using some of Freud's

practical techniques of dream analysis and free association separated out from Freud's materialistic and atheistic philosophy. But the reason I'm not too enthusiastic about Zen and TM is practical: they don't seem to work as well for most Christians as other, more personal forms of prayer. Zen is pretty difficult, and TM seems more of a psychological technique for calming and clarifying your mind than a way to pray. It's maybe a good thing in itself, but I don't think it's prayer. Perhaps it's the same kind of preliminary to prayer that psychoanalysis can be: it can clear away obstacles, mental garbage. If it helps, judged by Christian standards, I see no reason to forbid it. But I don't think we should spend our prayer time doing TM, using it as a substitute for prayer. And here's a very serious warning: if you do use it, be sure you separate it from its Hindu background and from the organization that makes you offer fruit and flowers to the Maharishi's dead guru and charges you for your mantra. The mantra, by the way, is usually the name of a Hindu god or goddess, but they don't tell you that! It's also a financial rip-off, I think. Dr. Berne and other scientists seemed to show you could get many similar results for free with any word at all for your own mantra. (He's the one who wrote *The Relaxation Response.*) I think the mantra's largely mystification, and also a concealed worship of a Hindu god.

Sal: I don't want to fly off into mystification, away from reality. And I certainly don't want to worship a false god. But I do want to practice Christian contemplative prayer. How do I answer the objection a lot of people have against contemplative prayer? They say all mysticism is just mystification and not realistic.

Chris: It's the most realistic thing in the world.

Sal: How do you figure that?

Chris: It's living in reality, conforming your mind to reality instead of living in fantasy. Most people

Contemplation is reality.

live in the supreme fantasy of a world without God. Contemplation lives in the real world, the world with God present.

Sal: That's a remarkably simple definition of contemplation.

Chris: Simple definitions are the best ones.

Sal: So contemplation is just awareness of God.

Chris: Yes.

Sal: And it's the mind that's aware, right?

Chris: Right. Not the calculating mind, of course, but the seeing mind.

Sal: But the will has to command the mind to turn to God, doesn't it?

Chris: Yes.

Sal: So it's a deliberate focusing of my attention on God. But that's something *I* have to do. But the great writers say it's not our effort but God's, that in contemplation we're receptive rather than active.

Chris: The *beginning* of it is active: our deliberate, willed turning the mind to God. It doesn't just happen, like a thunderstorm. You have to want it, will it. But just willing it won't produce it. God does. The writers you read are right: it's God who gives the gift. We're on the receiving end. But that's not only true of contemplation; that's true of all our knowledge of God. Unless he takes the initiative and reveals himself, we can't know him.

Sal: Is that necessarily so?

Chris: Yes. "No man has seen God at any time. The only begotten Son, who is in the bosom of the Father, he has made him known."

How we cooperate with God   *Sal:* So in all prayer, including contemplation, our will and God's will have to cooperate? We start it, and God finishes it? We ask, and he answers?

Chris: Not quite. You mustn't think we do 50 percent and God 50 percent, or even that we do 1 percent and God does 99 percent.

Sal: God does 100 percent?

Chris: Yes, but so do we!

Sal: I don't understand.

Chris: God does 100 percent, but that doesn't mean there's nothing left for us to do, because what God does is to work through us, not by magic, not against our will or even without it. He energizes our will.

Sal: That sounds like good theology, but what practical difference does it make to my prayer?

Chris: When you pray to God to give you grace— when you say to God, "I can't do this; I need You" —when you say that, you shouldn't then just sit back passively and do nothing. It's true that we can't do it without God, but it's also true that God won't do it without us.

Sal: The "it" here is contemplative prayer?

Chris: The "it" here is all forms of prayer, *and* overcoming sin, *and* being saved in the first place. All these things are God's grace, and yet they're our choice too. And it's not 50-50 either. God's grace is what energizes our free choice to ask for and accept his grace. And our free choice is the form his grace takes in us. They're two things, yet they're one.

Sal: That's a mystery, all right, how the same thing can be his *and* ours, and not 50-50.

Chris: Yes. But it makes sense. It's a little like an author and a character: How much of what Hamlet is and says and does is Hamlet, and how much is Shakespeare? It's all Hamlet, *and* it's all Shakespeare.

Sal: You've answered my questions, all right, in theory. But I still find it very difficult in practice to contemplate. I've tried it, and I've gotten nothing out of it.

Chris: I don't believe that's true.

Getting something out of it

Sal: What?

Chris: Did you put something into it?

Sal: I sure did.

Chris: Then you got something out of it: you pleased God by your effort. Isn't that what you want to do most of all? To please him rather than getting something for yourself?

Sal: Yes. I guess so.

Chris: If you had to choose between a prayer that pleased you but not God and a prayer that pleased God but not you, which would you choose?

Sal: To please God, of course.

Chris: Good. Then your attempt at contemplative prayer was not a failure, but a success, even though you didn't feel anything.

Sal: I believe that, but I still feel dissatisfied.

Chris: That's natural. It's very hard for us not to go by our feelings first of all. How often haven't you heard the complaint "I don't get anything out of it" from people who don't go to church anymore?

Sal: What do you say to them?

Chris: That if the only reason they went to church in the first place was "to get something out of it" for themselves rather than to give God the worship and praise and adoration he deserves, then I'm glad they stopped going.

Sal: I'll bet they're surprised to hear that!

Chris: Yes, and when they ask why, I say because the way to start doing a thing for the right reason is often to first stop doing it for the wrong reason.

Sal: You're right. I won't stop doing contemplation just because I don't get emotional feedback. Or doing any other form of prayer, for that matter.

Chris: Good. In that case you *will* get the feedback.

Sal: You mean God will give it to me when he sees I'm not idolizing it?

Chris: Yes, and also that you get the special joy of contemplative prayer only by forgetting yourself altogether.

Sal: The mystics say that we totally forget ourselves in God, just lose ourselves in God. Can we really do that?

Do you lose yourself in God?

Chris: Do what? How do you understand "lose ourselves in God"?

Sal: Lose your ego, or see through it as unreal?

Chris: Certainly not. If there's nobody there, who's doing the losing? If the ego were an illusion, who's seeing through the illusion? How could the gift of self be really given if the giver weren't real?

Sal: What do you lose, then? I thought they said you lose your very self.

Chris: They mean self-consciousness, self-regard, self-will, selfishness. You forget yourself. That's why it's so joyful. All joy is self-forgetful. You lose yourself— I mean your self-consciousness—in the other person, or the music, or the sunset, or the victory. But then the little shadow of self-regard comes and messes up the joy.

Sal: Is that all I am? A messy little shadow?

The problem of self-consciousness

Chris: No, no. You're the real I, the self, the image of God, whose name is I Am. The shadow is self-*consciousness*.

Sal: I understand *that* joy is unself-conscious, but I don't understand *why* that should be so, then. If my I is so great, why does remembering it mess up my joy?

Chris: It's like in the movies: the projector shouldn't be seen as part of the screen. If it is—if part of it is hanging loose, say, and blocking part of the lens—then the picture is messed up. You see, the projector isn't designed to project itself, but to project the movie. Well, we're like that projector. We were designed by God to know and love and praise and enjoy him and his other children and his world. Instead, we keep getting in our own way. Selfishness and self-regard are like pieces of self, pieces of the projector hanging down and blocking the light. They get in the way of what we're designed to do. In self-forgetfulness—in contemplative prayer and in love—we approach our original design, at least a little closer, for a little while. That's why it feels joyful: because whenever we do what we were designed to do, whenever we fulfill our nature as God designed it, we experience natural joy. That's why loving people makes us happy and hating them doesn't. Just as the body feels good when it's natural and healthy and feels bad when it's unnatural and diseased, or when it's doing something it's not designed to do, something contrary to its nature, like eating dirt.

A simple and practical method

Sal: O.K., now comes the practical question: How should I do it? Do you have a simple and practical method?

Chris: You've read some of the saints and mystics, haven't you?

Sal: Yes, and I'm a bit cowed by them.

Chris: Why?

Sal: Well, they teach you methods, but they're all pretty advanced and pretty complicated. Is contemplation complicated, really?

Chris: No, it's extremely simple, and most contemplatives say so.

Sal: But their *writing* about it isn't short and simple.

Chris: Then let's let ours be short and simple. The fundamental method, the way to contemplation, is simply to want it, to ask God for it, and to trust God for it. You see, it's a grace, not a piece of spiritual technology. So you can't force it. It's not "do-it-yourself mysticism". You have to ask God for it, and if God wants you to have it, he'll give it to you. If he doesn't, he won't.

Sal: So I won't necessarily get what I ask for.

Chris: You want God's will above all things, don't you?

Sal: Yes.

Chris: Then you'll get what you ask for; you'll get what you most want. You wouldn't want *anything* if it wasn't his will for you, would you?

Sal: Nope.

Chris: Then you'll get what you want. O.K.?

Sal: O.K.

Chris: Now, once you've said O.K. to that, and only then, I'll give you some advice on how to try to contemplate, some techniques you can use. But I had to be sure you weren't falling into the trap of spiritual technologism. Do you understand?

Sal: Yes. I'll treat whatever technique you tell me as an experiment. It doesn't *have* to work. There's only "one thing necessary".

Chris: Great. O.K., here's my simple method. There are just three things for you to do. First, purify your heart, then purify your mind, then just be there with God.

Sal: What does it mean to purify the heart?

Chris: Kierkegaard says, "Purity of heart is to will one thing." The heart is what wills, what loves. Purity of heart is to will only what God wills.

Sal: And how do I do that?

Chris: By willing to! There's no gimmick. But you could just repeat "Thy will be done" and mean it 100 percent. I like to call this "the prayer of yes".

Sal: That's a great little word.

Chris: Yes. It's like a password. Your will is the gate-keeper to your mind, your consciousness. Once your will is pure, the second step, your mind, will follow.

Sal: But only the saints are pure.

Chris: Not even them—and they're more aware of that than anyone.

Sal: I see now why it's so hard to pray this simplest of all prayers, this one word: because *I'm* not simple. I don't love God with all my heart, all my will. I *want* to—more than anything else in the world. But I don't. I have a divided will. I love myself and the world more than God sometimes.

Chris: As I said before, welcome to the human race. If you never loved yourself above God, you'd never have sinned. And welcome also to the company of the saints. Because they all say exactly the same thing about themselves. They all had the same difficulty praying the perfect prayer, the prayer of yes, that you have.

Sal: How did they do it then?

Chris: Only by God's grace. We're all spiritual crip-ples, sin addicts, handicapped children. But our Father loves us anyway, loves every one of his poor, crippled children, us just as much as the greatest saints. He won't deny us any of the grace, any of the help he gave them. He doesn't play favorites; he loves all his children, each one infinitely, totally. You too.

Sal: Why am I not a saint then?

Chris: The English writer William Law answered that. He said, "If you honestly consult your own heart you will find that there is one and only one reason why you are not now a saint: because you do not wholly want to be one."

Sal: That's true! And embarrassingly simple. . . . But now I'm in a double-bind, a catch-22. I'm not a saint because I don't will it with my whole will, and I don't will it with my whole will because I'm not a saint. I'm like that man in the Gospel lying beside the pool, crippled: he couldn't get into the healing waters because he was crippled, and he was crippled because he couldn't get into the healing waters.

Sal: And the only answer is grace. God cuts through that vicious circle. He gives us all the graces we need, all the graces he gives the saints, in fact. We just don't respond to him as they do.

God's grace breaks through.

Sal: So he does his part, but we don't do ours.

Chris: Right. Saint Francis of Assisi's disciple, Brother Giles, asks this question: "Tell me, brother, who, think you, is the readier: our God to give grace, or we to receive it?"

Sal: I see. It's got to be God who's ready and we who aren't. So we make the difference, then? It's up to us? The light shines for everyone, but we can close our eyes or open them? Is that how it is?

Chris: No, that's 50-50. He doesn't force his grace on us against our free will, but our very free will doesn't exist apart from grace. Our ability to receive his grace is itself a grace. Saint Teresa says, simply, "It's all grace."

Sal: You sound really convinced by that.

Chris: Those were the dying words of the wisest man I ever knew.

Sal: Oh! That is profound—but can you translate it into practice? What difference does it make to our prayer?

Chris: We needn't worry and strain and focus on ourselves. We don't succeed in prayer by just trying harder, by pushing. Trust God's grace instead.

Sal: We shouldn't try harder?

Chris: The New Testament hardly ever uses the word "try". But hundreds of times it tells us to trust.

Sal: Why trusting instead of trying?

Chris: Trying implies that we can do it, that sanctity comes from our making. Trusting implies that it comes from God, that we can't do it.

Sal: It just *comes*?

Chris: We have to receive it.

Sal: How?

Chris: Faith. Believe. Trust. That's how we receive. Those four words are used equivalently in the New Testament. It says in John's Gospel, "To as many as *received* him, he gave power to become children of God, to those who *believed* in his name." Believing is receiving. Trusting is accepting the gift.

Sal: So a saint isn't somebody who tries harder, but somebody who trusts more.

Chris: Exactly!

Sal: Then, "Lord, I believe; help my unbelief."

Chris: That's the right prayer for us, all right. We need a faith lift.

Sal: But I don't think I'll ever be totally simple-hearted, totally trusting, like a little baby.

Chris: Not until heaven. But we can at least move a little closer to heaven now, can't we? And experience some foretastes of it? Or at least smell it, if not taste it. Even that is more precious than possessing and tasting the whole world.

Sal: O.K., let me summarize what I'm aiming at now: purity of mind through purity of heart, right?

Chris: Yes.

Sal: I'm still not perfectly clear how the one causes the other.

Chris: Because the mind follows the will. The will is like the gatekeeper, and the mind is like a mansion. Only those visitors that get past the gatekeeper get in. Why do you think some thoughts rather than others?

Because your gatekeeper let them in, consciously or unconsciously.

Sal: I see. That's why we usually think pleasant thoughts rather than painful ones.

Chris: Or useful, practical, worthwhile, successful ones, instead of useless, impractical, worthless, unsuccessful ones. We *want* these.

Sal: And the practical application of this principle of psychology to prayer is . . . ?

Chris: That instead of any set of complicated mental methods or mental gymnastics, as some books advise, all you really have to do is one thing, "the one thing necessary", the thing Mary chose.

The one thing necessary

Sal: And that was Jesus, right?

Chris: Right. Martha thought about a thousand little worldly things because she chose to. She didn't have to. She probably gave that as an excuse: "*Somebody* has to worry about these things. My lazy sister left me with the dishes just to listen to Jesus. So I *have* to do the dishes." No, you *don't* have to do the dishes. You don't *have* to do *anything*. There's only "one thing necessary".

Sal: And after Mary's will chose Jesus first, how did her mind follow?

Chris: She sat at Jesus' feet and listened to him. And so can you.

Sal: And that happens in contemplative prayer, right? We hear his voice?

Chris: Yes, when you're quiet. Of course, his voice isn't usually physical; you sense his will and his love and his leadings.

Sal: That must be a terribly precious thing: to know you're addressed personally by Jesus.

Chris: You don't need contemplative prayer to know that. He told us all that: "I have called you by name." We can all know that by faith. The "experiences" or "sensible consolations" in prayer don't *add* anything to faith. No new, private revelations. If you think that's what you're getting, then it's probably from you, not from him.

Sal: But the listening does give us a direction, a leading, a guidance, doesn't it?

Chris: Yes. But that's a by-product; if you make it your primary goal, it won't work.

Sal: What do you mean?

Chris: If you go to Jesus just for the sake of getting something from him, even if it's a good thing like guidance for life, then you'll find neither him nor his guidance. If you sit at his feet only for his words, not for him, then you won't hear his words.

Sal: So I should go to him in contemplative prayer just as Mary did: just for him.

Chris: Yes. Just his presence. Just to be there with him, even if absolutely nothing "happens". Just giving him that time is enough. Because that's giving, not getting. That's love. That's seeking him alone, not him as a means to his gifts. The "seek and you shall find" promise applies to him, but not to anything else. Only one thing is absolutely guaranteed: the thing we all need more than anything else in the world, Jesus himself.

Sal: So I should just sit and listen, like Mary, and try to hear him just because it's him.

Chris: Yes, but don't *strain* to hear him.

Sal: Why not?

Not straining to hear *Chris:* Because it won't work. The act of trying so hard puts so much "noise" into the situation that that's the only thing you'll be able to hear. You get in your own way that way—like sticking your head out from behind the curtains to see the play better—you can't see the original play because you've changed it by inserting yourself into it. There's a scientist named

Heisenberg who says we can't see subatomic particles as they really are for that reason: the act of observing their position gets in the way of observing their true velocity, or the act of observing their velocity gets in the way of observing their true position. He called it his "Uncertainty Principle".

Sal: I'm not sure I understand that. . . .

Chris: Frankly, I'm not sure anyone else does either!

Sal: But I shouldn't deliberately try hard to listen, right?

Chris: Right.

Sal: So after I get my will single and my mind single and send my mind to Jesus' feet, what do I do there?

Chris: Nothing. Just be there. Don't move. Let him call the shots.

Sal: I guess he's better at it than I am, so that makes sense. You know, the method you gave me makes me feel free—free of methods. The books I read offered so many methods, and such complicated ones, that I was about to give up hope. But this is easy.

Chris: It's very easy to understand. But it's not easy to do.

Sal: Isn't there a way of making it easier?

Chris: No! That would just be more methods again, more complications. At some point or other, you just have to *do* it. Even if the method has twelve steps, you have to start the first step. So I've cut through all the steps and said, "just do it". No method, no means to *that* end, no road to *that* goal. At some point, you *just do it*. So let's make that the very first point. When the one you love is knocking at the door, you don't worry about methods and steps in the process of getting up and opening the door; you just do it.

Sal: And it's like that here, isn't it? The one we love *is* knocking on the door of our hearts.

Chris: And all we have to do is open the door, and then he comes in and eats with us, and we with him. That's his promise too. (That's Revelation 3:20.) *That's* what contemplative prayer is good for.

Dialogue Ten

How to See God Everywhere

Sal: Chris, I think I've found the biggest problem of all in prayer.

Chris: What's that?

Sal: Everything else! I mean, there are problems *in* prayer, all right, but the biggest problem is outside of prayer: the rest of my life.

Chris: You mean prayer doesn't make as big a difference to the rest of your life as it should?

Sal: Exactly. How do I remember God during the day?

Chris: How do you try to?

Sal: I try using gimmicks occasionally, like notes or time reminders, but it seems artificial.

Chris: It works for some people—like praying for a minute every hour on the hour.

Sal: That's not enough. What about the other fifty-nine minutes?

Chris: I'm glad you make that demand, Sal.

Sal: I don't want compliments. I want answers.

Chris: And you'll get them. From God, if not from me, because he promised, remember?

Sal: "Seek and you shall find" again?

Chris: Yes. What you're seeking is simply God. And that's what he promised to give you.

Sal: All right, how? He usually works through natural things, through things and people rather than miracles. Maybe he'll give me an answer through you. What's your answer to my problem?

Chris: Let's get the problem fully stated first, O.K.?

Bringing prayer into life

Sal: Fine. It's this separation of God and my life, God and my work. I can bring my life into my prayer, but I don't know how to bring prayer into my life and my work. I used to pray mechanically, and now God is really present in my prayer. But I still *work* mechanically, and God doesn't seem to be present in my work.

Chris: That's a wonderful complaint, Sal!

Sal: And that's a pretty weird compliment! How can a complaint be wonderful?

Chris: If it's what God wants. You're seeking a very good thing: in fact, God himself in your life. Therefore you are guaranteed to find it, guaranteed by God himself.

Sal: "Seek and you shall find" again, right?

Chris: Yes. Be assured you're on the right road. You're in the right school, even if you're only in the first grade. You're in God's school of prayer.

Sal: I believe that. But I want to know what the lessons are. How do I graduate? How do I learn how to see God everywhere in my life? To remember him during a busy day? To keep that closeness all day, not just during prayer time?

Chris: "Closeness"—do you mean *feeling* close to God?

Staying close to God

Sal: No. I know feelings change. I know I shouldn't rely on feelings. I mean *being* close. Willing his will. Offering everything in my life to him. Letting him make a difference to everything in my life. He's God, after all. I can't confine him to a church, or to a fifteen-minute prayer! He's got to make a difference to everything in my life. I want to carry him around with me, like Mary at the visitation to Elizabeth—carry the silence, the place of peace, the Prince of Peace, into all places, hidden in me like a baby.

Chris: That's what you want most?

Sal: Yes.

Chris: Then once again, the promise certainly applies to you. Seekers find. You'll get what you want.

Sal: I certainly hope so.

Chris: What kind of hope? A wish or a certainty? An unsure hope or a sure one?

Sal: Why do you ask?

Chris: Because you must be certain at the beginning. It can't be an experiment; it has to be a certainty, holding God to his promise. Unless you move in faith, you won't move.

Sal: Why?

Chris: Because this is a lifelong, twenty-four-hour-a-day thing you're undertaking. You can't give yourself any escape hatch. You can't even entertain the *possibility* of giving up. So I have to ask how certain you are that this is no "pie-in-the-sky-by-and-by" dream but something God commands here and now.

Sal: I'm sure of that.

Chris: Why? What's the ground of your faith?

Sal: God's Word: "Whether you eat, or drink, or whatsoever you do, do all to the glory of God." If God commanded it, it must be done. And Jesus did it, and he's our model. *He*'s not pie-in-the-sky-by-and-by.

Do all to the glory of God.

Chris: Good! That's the firm foundation, all right.

Sal: And I also believe that it's got to be done not just inside our heads but in the material world; that work has to *be* a prayer, somehow, not just that we can interrupt our work for prayer every now and then.

Chris: Good! You're profoundly right there too. How do you know that's true?

Sal: Because of the creation and the Incarnation—the two greatest events in history. God made matter, and God became matter. Therefore matter is holy. Every speck of dust is holy. He made it all, and he owns it all. And when he became a man, he became that dust. God got dirt under his fingernails. God worked in a little carpenter's shop. There's nothing that's secular. Everything is sacred, because God is everywhere. I *know* that. But how do I *see* him everywhere? That's my question. I want to hear him say to me from everything in the world, "This is my body", and from every pain and suffering and death, "This is my blood."

Chris: Well, you certainly have a good and noble goal there.

Sal: I don't think it's *noble*, really. It's just *sane*. I mean, I just want to live in the real world, in the truth. I don't want to play nice little games and create my own little world inside my own head. If God *is* everywhere, I want to live as if he is, just because he is. And if he's not, then Christianity is a lie.

Chris: You've learned the lesson of honesty well, Sal. Congratulations.

Sal: Thanks, but I came to you for practical suggestions, not congratulations. *How* do I do this?

Chris: How *do* you do it? Now, I mean. What attempts have you made?

Sal: Well, for one thing, fifteen minutes often seems too short now. At first it seemed too long. But expanding the fifteen minutes is no solution, even if it got expanded to twenty-four hours. I don't want just *more* prayer; I want a different kind of prayer: the kind I can bring into my day, my work, my life.

Chris: What else do you try?

Sal: I try to remember. But I forget.

Chris: You can't *consciously* remember God all the time. He doesn't expect you to. And of course you needn't worry that he forgets you when you forget him.

Sal: I also try to begin every day with him. I wait till I'm more fully awake to do my fifteen-minute prayer, but as soon as I wake up I try to "think God", to give him the first minute, anyway.

Beginning the day with God

Chris: How does that work?

Sal: It's surprisingly hard. As soon as I wake up, it feels as if a thousand little soldiers start attacking me: thoughts about the day, plans, and details, and obligations. I have to shove them aside ruthlessly if I want to pray first. They seem jealous of my prayer time, even fifteen seconds. They seem to be trying to make me put them first, not God. They seem to say to me, "You're too busy to pray today." And I try to remember the answer to that: "I'm too busy *not* to pray today. The busier I am, the more I need prayer."

Chris: And when you succeed, what happens?

Sal: Sometimes it feels like a spy reporting for duty, getting my assignment, my secret mission for the day from my commander. It makes the day exciting and important, gives it a purpose.

Chris: And what do you usually pray then? Anything special?

Sal: When I'm still sleepy, I need the formulas, the good crutches. So I start with a morning prayer, a morning offering of my day to God. And I try to rest for just a few seconds in his arms, to remind myself where I am, where I'm coming from before I go everywhere else.

Chris: Sounds like an excellent start.

Sal: But that's all. The only ways I can remember him regularly during the day are silly and artificial. I'm sure he doesn't want me to sanctify my day by leaving little notes around, or by putting two candles in the bathroom!

Chris: No, but I'm going to suggest some things that will sound artificial at first, but they can become natural, habitual. (Habit is called "second nature", you know.)

Sal: Suggest away!

Chris: You know God is with you every moment, right?

Sal: Right.

Chris: But it's hard to bring that abstract truth into connection with your concrete world, right?

Sal: Right. What can do that?

Chris: Imagination can do that. Myths did that for millions of years for millions of people. Jesus' parables did it.

Sal: And how am I to use my imagination?

Chris: My suggestion is based on the Incarnation. We can't imagine God the Father, pure spirit. But we can imagine God the Son. He has a human body. Right?

Sal: Right.

Chris: So simply imagine Jesus Christ at your side wherever you go.

Sal: Physically?

Chris: Yes, physically. It has to be physically. It has to be concrete, not abstract. For instance, keep an empty chair next to you when you sit down. That's Jesus' chair. It reminds you that he's really there, just as really as you are. You believe that, don't you?

Sal: Yes.

Chris: You can't see him, but you *can* see his chair. So the chair helps you to remember him, to remember the truth.

Sal: I see.

Chris: And when you're walking, imagine he's always at your right side—not just "at your side" in the abstract, but at the *right* side, concretely, physically, always in the same place, always on the same side. That's Jesus' side. Sometimes he goes ahead of you, to lead you where he wants you to go. And sometimes he stays behind, when you go where he doesn't want you to go. That reminds you that you're his follower, that you should follow wherever he leads.

Sal: I see. "Leading and following" can be made concrete. But isn't that *too* concrete? Isn't that superstitious and pagan and materialistic?

Chris: Why do you think God gave us bodies? And a material world? As a mistake? Or to use them as roads to meet him on? I honestly don't think there's much danger of becoming superstitious about it and taking it literally. You're just not that stupid. I think there's far more danger of the opposite extreme.

Sal: What's that?

Chris: A kind of angelism, abstractionism, bad spiritualism.

Sal: That's true. I have more of a problem making God concretely real than making him spiritual. The problem isn't that he's too close to matter, but too far removed from it.

Chris: And it's theologically correct too, because he *is* incarnate.

God is still incarnate.

Sal: *Was,* you mean.

Chris: He still has his human nature and his human body now, in heaven—the body Thomas touched, the body that ate with his disciples after he rose from the dead. That's the clear teaching of Scripture and the creeds.

Sal: That's true.

Chris: And we're his body, too, the Church. Where is our Head? Floating somewhere up above his body? Are we beheaded?

Sal: No. He promised he'd be with us always.

Chris: And he is. Once he married matter, there could be no divorce.

Sal: O.K. I'm convinced. Do you have any more specific suggestions?

Chris: Here's a very simple one that works best when you combine it with the first one. Chat with Jesus during the day, as friend to friend. Aloud. That's important. Vague, wordless thoughts and feelings usually dissipate, like steam. Use concrete words, not abstract thoughts and feelings. Whispered, maybe, but spoken.

Sal: You could chat with him even without the chair and the right side, couldn't you?

Chris: Yes, but you can see how it works better if you see him there with you, really present, right here and now, not far away.

Sal: Just chatting about anything, right?

Chris: Anything and everything. He's interested in it all, you know. Everything about you. Just as when you're passionately in love with someone, you're interested in every little detail about that person. And his love for us is infinite. So don't ever think anything is too small or ugly for him.

Sal: Do you think the conversations should be long or short?

Chris: Either. Sometimes just a phrase: just turn to him and say, "Thank you, Jesus", or "I love you, Jesus", or "I do this for love of you, Jesus", whenever the Spirit moves you.

Sal: I can see how this could bring about a really powerful change in my life. It's like being one of his disciples, walking with him every day, everywhere.

Chris: That *is* what discipleship is. *Discipleship*

Sal: Everything I've heard or read about "discipleship" sounded more general and abstract and vague. This makes it real—real presence!

Chris: No, this doesn't *make* it real. It *is* real. *He* has already made it real. This exercise just lives in reality. It's supremely realistic. Unless Jesus is a liar. He promised to be with us always, until the end of the world. Do you think he's less real, less present, less powerful than you imagine? Or more?

Sal: More. More than I *can* imagine.

Chris: All right, then. That's the suggestion for the whole day. Now let's see if we can divide the day into parts and find a kind of prayer for each part, O.K.?

Sal: O.K. But my life doesn't go by regular schedules. My day isn't divided into neat parts.

Chris: I didn't mean that way. I meant that every- *Basic parts of life* body's life is divided into basic parts or dimensions.

Sal: Like what?

Chris: Life and death, for one thing.

Sal: O.K.

Chris: And joys and sorrows.

Sal: Right.

Chris: And waking and sleeping.

Sal: Yes.

Chris: And when we're awake, we're usually either sitting, walking, or standing, right?

Sal: Right.

Chris: So that gives us ten areas: work, play, joy, sorrow, sitting, walking, standing, sleeping, living, and dying. I think we can find an answer to your need in each one. Let's start with working. You know the principle, don't you, that work can be, itself, a form of prayer? That we can and should work for God, as well as praying to God? That our work is a divine calling, a vocation, whether we're missionaries or garbagemen? That every work is equally from God and for God?

Praying in our work **Sal:** I believe that. But how do you "practice the presence of God" during work?

Chris: I know of two different ways. One of them offers the act of working to God, the other offers the finished product.

Sal: How do you offer the act?

Chris: We usually work for our own sake, for our benefit, for the rewards of the work. Sometimes that's money, sometimes it's pleasure, like eating food we cooked or wearing clothes we mended. We usually work for ourselves. If we didn't hope for the reward, we wouldn't work. Isn't that so?

Sal: Yes.

Chris: What we want to do now is to change our motive, not our work. Instead of looking ahead at the reward and anticipating our pleasure in getting it, try looking back at God who gave you the work. Look at the roots instead of the fruits of your work. Look at your work as a deed directed by God, like a part in a play, or a step in a dance, or a song. God's the author. We act *from him*, instead of *for ourselves*. Incidentally, that also frees us from fear of failure and from compulsion to succeed. Our act of working can be simply a response to God instead of a need to satisfy our desires—doing it because he wills it. And if he doesn't, then we shouldn't be doing it anyway.

Sal: Do you mean our careers, our jobs, are his vocation, or every little thing, like picking up a pin?

Chris: Everything. You can pick up a pin for God, for the love of God.

Sal: Practically, really, literally?

Chris: Yes. This has been tried. This works.

Sal: By great saints?

Chris: By ordinary people. A little bit at first, then more and more, developing into a habit, a "second nature".

Sal: I'll try it. And what's the other way?

Chris: To offer up your finished product to God, not just the act of working and your inner intention. To do the very best job you possibly can because it's not just for yourself or for other people but for God. How well would you write a letter if Jesus was going to read it? How good a job would you do repairing a car if you knew Jesus was going to drive it? *Offering up the results of work*

Sal: Oh—and that's not an "if", either, is it? Because he said to us, "Insofar as you have done it to one of the least of these my brothers, you have done it to me." So both the working and the work, the act and the product, can be a prayer. That's work. What about play? That seems harder to find God in.

Chris: Why?

Sal: Because work is serious business, and so is God. But play is stepping back from serious business. So it looks like stepping back from God.

Chris: Do you think God doesn't play? Do you think he's all business? All seriousness?

Sal: I never thought of God as playing.

Chris: Didn't you ever look at an ostrich?

Sal: That's a good answer. But is that good theology?

Chris: It sure is. God always plays. Even creating the world was play for him, not work. All he had to do was speak, and it was. No sweat, literally. *God and play*

Sal: You mean God is all play and no work?

Chris: I mean the two are the same for him. For us they're opposites. But of the two, play is the better image for God's activity, because our work always has an end beyond itself—work is always *for* something else—but play is for its own sake.

Sal: I guess heaven's work will be play for us too, won't it?

Chris: Yes. C. S. Lewis says, "Joy is the serious business of heaven."

Sal: So play is heavenly.

Chris: Yes. And therefore it can be a prayer, because it's godlike, it images God.

Sal: Isn't this emphasis on play sort of childish and irresponsible?

Chris: Only if it's an excuse for not working. We need both.

Sal: So, concretely, how do we pray as we play?

Chris: By remembering that play is a foretaste of heaven. As you catch a little of the sun in the sunbeam, you catch a little of God's play in our play. You run back up the sunbeam to the sun.

Sal: What do you mean by that?

God is made of joy. *Chris:* You can play to God because play is from God. You can praise him in play, and thank him for play, and enjoy him in the play. He's there too. It's God we enjoy in playing, you know, just as it's sunlight we enjoy in sunbeams. God is *made* of joy, so all our enjoyments are revelations of God.

Sal: Even sinful ones?

Chris: They're perversions of something good. That's the only way they can attract us: by promising some sort of joy. Joy, as such, is good. We miss an awful lot if we don't find God in our joys.

Sal: We've gone from "play" to "joy" as if they're the same thing. Are they?

Chris: Not quite. Play is something we do, and joy is something we experience when we play. But also when we work. So joy is broader than play.

Sal: Do you have two different prayers, then, one for play and one for joy?

Chris: When you play, just remember you're playing with God, romping with God.

Sal: Isn't that a little disrespectful?

Chris: No. God's our Father, after all. We're his babies. What loving father doesn't want to share his baby's little games and play and romp with him?

Sal: So God is really interested in little league baseball.

Chris: Yes. More than we are.

Sal: Isn't he bored?

Chris: God's never bored.

Sal: Why not?

Chris: Because he's infinite love. Love is the thing that makes things enjoyable for us too. If that's your baby and you love him, you're not bored playing peek-a-boo with him.

Sal: O.K., so the prayer of play is to remember that we're playing with God and that God is playing with us and enjoying it as much as we are.

Chris: More!

Sal: All right. What's the prayer for joy?

Chris: Tracing the sunbeam back up to the sun. Seeing God in all joys. Thanking God for the little pieces of heaven that he lets fall to earth. (Chicken Little was right, you know: the sky is falling. All the time.)

Sal: All right, let's look at sorrow next. How do I pray *Prayer in sorrow* in sorrow? I've known or read about some Christians who seem pretty good at finding God in sorrow but not in joy, and others who find him in joy but not in sorrow. Isn't it hard to do both?

Chris: No. Look at Jesus. He's completely human. It's we who are lopsided, one way or another.

Sal: So what can we do with sorrow?

Chris: Offer it up.

Sal: What does that mean?

Chris: Give it to God, to use as he pleases.

Sal: How can God use sorrows and sufferings?

Chris: He used Jesus' sufferings to save the whole human race.

Sal: I don't understand how that works.

Chris: No one understands just *how* it works. We don't even understand how gravity works, or why it works. But we know it does. And we know that our sufferings "work" too, because we're in his body. Our sufferings share in his work. The Bible clearly teaches that.

Offering our suffering to God

Sal: So the prayer in suffering can be: "This is for you, Lord; do with it what you will."

Chris: Yes. In union with Christ, "in Christ".

Sal: That's easy to say and hard to do, you know. When you're suffering, you don't usually feel like praying.

Chris: I know. That's why those prayers are especially precious: they come from the depths, not the surface; the will, not the feelings.

Sal: So the prayer in sorrow is just to offer it up to God, hoping he'll make something good of it?

Chris: No, *knowing* he will. That's a promise: "All things work together for good for those who love God." That's why we can do more than just offer it up to God. We can even praise him for it.

Sal: Praise God for suffering?

Chris: Not for being the author of it, but for allowing us to help him make something good out of it, yes. We're Jesus' assistant garbagemen. We continue the job he did. He got his hands dirty taking out the world's garbage, and we're his hands now.

Sal: And what is he making out of all this terrible suffering?

Chris: Something "eye has not seen, ear has not heard, nor has it entered into the heart of man". We just have to trust him.

Sal: I think it's easy for most people to believe he has *some* reason for allowing them to suffer; if they don't believe that, their suffering becomes meaningless. But to praise him in the middle of suffering—that takes a much stronger faith. That doesn't seem reasonable to most people.

Chris: But it is, if you believe God's Word. Remember, "*all* things work together for good". Therefore, "in *everything* give thanks". And it *is* reasonable: if God is all-loving and all-powerful, then everything he does is good and therefore praiseable, even allowing us to suffer, even as he allowed his Son to suffer. It's all for good. It doesn't begin in good, it begins in evil. But it can end in good. Suffering began in the fall, but it ends in redemption. We're on the road. Our pains are growing pains.

All things work together for good.

Sal: You say suffering doesn't begin in God. Doesn't everything? Isn't he the Creator of everything?

Chris: No. We create some things too: our choices. He created us with free will. We really begin something new when we choose; we don't just transmit lines of heredity and environment. And we're the ones who create evil.

Sal: So sin is the origin of suffering?

Chris: That's what Genesis says. If our souls were perfectly in line with God, our bodies and our world would be too. Once we rebelled against our designer, his design for us fell apart in us.

Sal: And how does God take suffering—the result of sin—and use it for good—the opposite of sin?

Chris: I don't know *how* he does it, anymore than a cat knows how we make airplanes. But I know *that* he does.

Sal: If only we could see it!

Chris: We see it in Jesus, where the most evil deed ever done—the murder of God—was for our salvation. The world killed God, and God saved the world by it. We celebrate this most terrible tragedy of all time as *Good* Friday. If he can make even *that* evil work for good, then he can make our little evils work for good too.

Sal: And the practical point of all this deep theology for prayer is . . . ?

Chris: That we can pray in confidence that Infinite Love is in complete control even now. "He's got the whole world in his hands." He knows what he's doing. So we can trust him and even praise him even as he lets us suffer, because *he* lets us suffer. We're not praising or glorifying suffering, but him. Even in great pain we can still mutter, "I trust you, Jesus. You were here too."

Sal: But we're also told to pray "deliver us from evil".

Chris: Yes. That's what he's doing, but in his time and his way. It's a little like a dog caught in a bear trap: he has to trust his master even when he hurts him by moving the trap, because he knows he's getting him out. He trusts him.

Sal: So we can pray "praise the Lord" and "deliver us from evil" at the same time?

Chris: Yes.

Sal: So we say both "yes" and "no" to suffering.

Chris: Yes. If we only say "no", we feel resentment, desperation, frustration, failure. If we only say "yes", we become passive and inhuman.

Sal: I see. And—more importantly—I see Jesus: he did what you say. He asked his Father before the cru- cifixion, "Let this cup of suffering pass from me." He prayed, "Deliver me from evil." But he also accepted it when it came. So what you say is founded on him. That settles it. I'll do it. It's his way.

Chris: I'm glad you settled it before doing it. Prayers aren't scientific experiments. A skeptical attitude is right for science—"Try it, see if it works." But it's wrong for personal relationships, wrong for love.

Sal: O.K. What's the next area of life to look at for a special kind of prayer?

Chris: Sleeping and waking.

Sal: Sleeping too, eh? How can we pray when we're asleep? *Prayer in sleeping*

Chris: Brother Lawrence says in *The Practice of the Presence of God*, "The gale of the Holy Spirit blows even in our sleep." God doesn't sleep just because we do, you know.

Sal: How can we pray when we're sleeping?

Chris: We can commit our sleep to God before we sleep, just as we can commit our death to God before we die. Sleep is an image of death, you know.

Sal: So this is the last prayer of the day?

Chris: Yes. Our last thought before we sleep should be God. We give him permission to enter our sleep, our dreams, our unconscious.

Sal: He needs *permission*?

Chris: He doesn't need it, but he wants it. He's a gentleman. He respects our freedom. He rarely takes what we don't give him. But when we do, when we turn over an area of our life to him, he takes it and starts to work there. We need him to work in our unconscious too. That part of us is even broader and deeper than our conscious, and it influences the conscious mind in powerful and hidden ways. How could we not want God there too?

Sal: Right you are. So we should fall asleep like a baby in Daddy's arms, right?

Chris: Exactly.

Sal: O.K., now let's look at waking.

Sitting meditation **Chris:** We divided it into sitting, walking, and standing. For sitting I had in mind some of the traditional ways of meditation that have worked well for centuries, sitting meditation.

Sal: Yoga, you mean? Isn't that Hindu?

Chris: Not necessarily, no. Let's not get hung up on the name. Many religions use means of quieting the mind by means of the body. Christians can too, up to a point.

Sal: What point?

Chris: Cultivating sheer emptiness, or trance. That opens you up to all sorts of spirits. We open ourselves up to God alone. Only if yoga does that is it good.

Sal: It's painful and difficult, though, isn't it?

Chris: Not at all. Four simple features of most forms of yoga are simple and easy for almost everyone. First, posture. Body and mind are so closely knit that quieting the body helps quiet the mind. So sit perfectly still and relaxed, but with a completely straight back —either on a straight chair or squatting on the floor. Second, breathing: breathe slowly and regularly, quietly, calmly. That's another body function that rubs off on the soul, so to speak. You can also use breathing to quiet your mind by concentrating on it for a while, thinking only of "in" and "out". It's God's air, you know, and it's the material thing that both Hebrew and Greek, the two languages of the Bible, use as a symbol of spirit: *ruah* in Hebrew and *pneuma* in Greek both mean both "breath" and "spirit". In a sense you're breathing God in and out. He's here, in you and out of you, he in you and you in him. You can concentrate on that in breathing. Third, there's body awareness. That sharpens and quiets your mind too. Just focus your awareness on different parts of your body, one by one. Notice each tiny sensation, from toes to ears. You'll be surprised how it wakes up your mind and, at the same time, takes away agitation and nervousness.

Finally, let all your thoughts pass through your mind and out; empty your mind. Think about nothing.

Sal: Isn't that dangerous?

Chris: Not if you begin by inviting God to come in. Not if you sweep the house of your mind clean for God. He tells us to do that, remember: "Be still and know that I am God." If we're not still, we can't hear him. And yoga helps some people to become still for him.

Sal: I see. So it's an aid to contemplative prayer.

Chris: Yes. It's quite simple, really. There are hundreds of books about it, but you don't need them, I think, as much as you need just to do it, to practice. I don't trust books much.

Sal: That's the sitting prayer. What's the walking prayer? *Walking prayer*

Chris: It's very simple. When you're walking, especially a long distance, remember where you're going.

Sal: What do you mean?

Chris: Heaven. "This world is not my home, I'm just a-passing through." If that isn't true, Christianity is simply false. And if it is true, we'd better remember it. How silly to travel without remembering where we're going! Walking is a good image of it, an easy reminder. The earthly place you're walking to is a way station to heaven.

Sal: I see. I heard a hymn about that that made a deep impression on me once, and I remembered the line: "One sweetly solemn thought/Comes to me o'er and o'er:/I'm one day nearer come today/Than I ever was before."

Chris: You understand, then. Let's look at a standing prayer next. *Standing prayer*

Sal: O.K.

Chris: It's for waiting in line, or any kind of waiting, which is usually standing. But it can be sitting too, like waiting in a doctor's office. It's really a waiting prayer. One of the hardest things to do is to wait—even for humans, much less for God. But "they also serve who only stand and wait". There's a remarkable book by Simone Weil called *Waiting for God*.

Sal: And how do we pray while we wait?

Chris: Just a simple prayer of faith and hope and love, like: "Lord, I believe this waiting is your will too, even though it seems like a waste of time. I believe you waste nothing, and you arranged this time for me, so I offer it to you." It doesn't matter so much what you choose to say, just that you get into the habit of using "wasted" time, waiting time, as a prayer.

Sal: O.K. What's left?

Life and death   *Chris:* Life and death. What I had in mind as the prayer of life was a simple thanksgiving for being born, for sheer existence. We don't usually notice big things like that. We're like ants in front of an elephant. The most important things are too big for us to notice most of the time. So we should remind ourselves of them. Especially in an age when being born is such a perilous business, when almost as many babies get aborted as born.

Sal: And that brings us to death. What does prayer have to do with death?

Chris: Prayer is a rehearsal for death, a little death. It's a death of self-will and egotism and playing God. When we pray, we die to our time and our will and our mind and let God's time and God's will and God's mind take their place. Prayer is dying to self, sinking into God.

Sal: I see. That's why it's so appropriate for the last prayer of the night, before I sleep, to be a yielding, a sinking into God, a losing of myself in him. He keeps it safe for the morning, as he keeps the self I lose in death safe for the resurrection and for heaven.

Chris: Exactly right, Sal. Death is God's hand too, taking us home, like a mother's call: "Come, little child; put away your toys now, it's time to come home." We can trust God even with our death: "Even though I walk through the valley of the shadow of death, . . . Thou art with me." He's been there first and made it safe for us. We can follow him even into the darkness. All prayer, but especially night prayer, is a little rehearsal for that, for the time when our whole life becomes one prayer offered up to God at our last moment, when we're finally complete, finished, like a story that's fully written and goes home to the printer.

Sal: Is there any other special prayer we can pray during the day that's a rehearsal for that last, great prayer, death? I'm not sure I want to do it, but I want to know what it is.

Rehearsing for death

Chris: Why aren't you sure you want to do it?

Sal: It just sounds a bit morbid to think of death during the day and during life when you're young and healthy.

Chris: The prayer I have in mind is just the opposite of morbid: it makes you more alive, makes you appreciate life much more.

Sal: By thinking of death?

Chris: Yes. It's using your imagination again. Imagine you have just one day to live, that this is your last day alive. They say, "Scarcity confers value." If you have only one day, it's precious. Notice things: how beautiful every blade of grass is, how precious every person is, how infinitely lovable, with all their faults.

Sal: If I thought I was going to die tomorrow, I'd tell a lot of people how important they were to me too. Maybe I'd better do that today.

Chris: Yes. Someday it will be too late. This is no fantasy: the one thing you can be absolutely sure of is that one day *will* be the last day of your life. This is a realistic prayer exercise.

Sal: And if I had one day to live, I wouldn't worry about trivia. I wouldn't be like the ant, who sees only little things and misses the big things because they're so close, like God. This would make me notice God, as well as the world and people.

Chris: It might be hard to keep it up for a whole day. But you could keep coming back to it, even after you forget. And repeating it makes it easier, habitual. Also, it could be a good five-minute prayer, or fifteen-minute prayer: imagine you have only five or only fifteen minutes to live: what would you say to God? There's nothing like impending death to sharpen your awareness.

Sal: It would make all other prayers clearer too. It's just the opposite of morbid. It makes everything in life clearly seen and precious.

Death as it *Chris:* Even death itself. If your life is full of prayer,
really is. full of God, then you see death as it really is.

Sal: As it really is?

Chris: Yes. Because of Jesus' descent into it, even death is holy. It's the golden chariot sent by the King to fetch us, his Cinderella bride, from the ashes, to take us home to marry him.

Sal: That's finally what it all comes down to, isn't it? What our whole life is? Once we've said "yes" instead of "no" to God, our whole life is a love story.

Chris: Yes. That's it.

Favorite Prayers

The Lord's Prayer

Our Father, who art in Heaven,
Hallowed be Thy name;
Thy kingdom come;
Thy will be done on earth as it is in Heaven.
Give us this day our daily bread;
and forgive us our trespasses
as we forgive those who trespass against us;
and lead us not into temptation,
but deliver us from evil.
For Thine is the kingdom, and the power,
and the glory now and forever. AMEN.

The Apostles' Creed

I believe in God, the Father almighty,
   Creator of Heaven and earth.
I believe in Jesus Christ, his only Son, Our Lord.
   He was conceived by the power of the Holy Spirit
   and born of the Virgin Mary.
He suffered under Pontius Pilate,
   was crucified, died, and was buried.
He descended to the dead.
On the third day He rose again.
He ascended into Heaven,
   and is seated at the right hand of the Father.
He will come again to judge the living and the dead.
I believe in the Holy Spirit,
   the holy catholic Church,

the communion of saints,
the forgiveness of sins,
the resurrection of the body,
and the life everlasting. AMEN.

The Doxology

Glory be to the Father, and to the Son, and to the Holy Spirit as it was in the beginning, is now, and will be forever. AMEN.

An Act of Faith

O God,
I firmly believe all the truths that You have revealed
and that You teach us through your Church,
for You are Truth itself
and can neither deceive nor be deceived.

An Act of Hope

O God,
I hope with complete trust that You will give me,
through the merits of Jesus Christ,
all necessary grace in this world
and everlasting life in the world to come,
for this is what You have promised
and You always keep Your promises.

An Act of Love

O God,
I love You with my whole heart above all things,
because You are infinitely good;
and for Your sake I love my neighbor as I love myself.

An Act of Contrition

O God,
I am sorry with my whole heart for all my sins
because You are Goodness itself
and sin is an offense against You.
Therefore I firmly resolve,
with the help of Your grace,
not to sin again and to avoid the occasions of sin.

A Confession of Sin

Almighty and most merciful Father,
We have erred, and strayed from Thy ways like lost sheep;
we have followed too much the devices and desires of our
    own hearts;
we have offended against Thy holy laws;
we have left undone those things which we ought to have
    done;
and we have done those things which we ought not to have
    done.
And there is no health in us.
But Thou, O Lord, have mercy on us, miserable offenders;
spare Thou those who confess their faults;
restore Thou those who are penitent,
according to Thy promises declared unto mankind in Christ
    Jesus, our Lord;
and grant, O most merciful Father, for His sake,
that we may hereafter live a godly, righteous and sober life
to the glory of Thy holy name. AMEN.

The Restless Heart

Thou hast made us for Thyself,
And our hearts are restless until they rest in Thee.

Saint Augustine

Day by Day

> May I know You more clearly,
> Love You more dearly,
> And follow You more nearly,
> Day by day.

Saint Richard of Chichester

Saint Patrick's Breastplate

Christ, be with me, Christ before me, Christ behind me.
Christ in me, Christ beneath me, Christ above me,
Christ on my right, Christ on my left,
Christ where I lie, Christ where I sit, Christ where I arise,
Christ in the heart of everyone who thinks of me,
Christ in the mouth of everyone who speaks of me,
Christ in every eye that sees me,
Christ in every ear that hears me.

Saint Ignatius' Gift

Lord, I freely yield to You all my liberty.
Take my memory, my intellect, and my entire will.
You have given me everything I am or have;
I give it all back to you to stand under your will alone.
Your love and Your grace are enough for me,
I ask for nothing more.

Saint Ignatius of Loyola

God Be in My Head

God be in my head and in my understanding.
God be in my eyes and in my looking.
God be in my mouth and in my speaking.
God be in my heart and in my thinking.
God be at my end and my departing.

For a Holy Heart

Lord, grant me a holy heart
that sees always what is fine and pure
and is not frightened at the sight of sin,
but creates order wherever it goes.
Grant me a heart that knows nothing of boredom, weeping
and sighing.
Let me not be too concerned with the bothersome thing I
call "myself".
Lord, give me a sense of humor,
and I will find happiness in life and profit for others.

Saint Thomas More

Prayer of Saint Francis

Lord, make me an instrument of your peace:
where there is hatred, let me sow love;
where there is injury, pardon;
where there is doubt, faith;
where there is despair, hope;
and where there is sadness, joy.
O Divine Master, grant that I may not seek so much
to be consoled as to console,
to be understood as to understand,
to be loved as to love.
For it is in giving that we receive,
it is in pardoning that we are pardoned,
and it is in dying that we are born to eternal life.

Saint Francis of Assisi

Canticle of the Sun

O most high, almighty, good Lord!
All praise, glory, honor, and exaltation are Yours.
To You alone do they belong,
and no mere mortal dares pronounce Your name.

Praise to You, O Lord our God, for all Your creatures:
first for our dear Brother Sun,
who gives us the day and illumines us with his light.
Fair is he, in splendor radiant,
bearing Your very likeness, O Lord.

For our Sister Moon
and for the bright, shining stars
we praise You, O Lord.

For our Brother Wind,
for fair and stormy seasons
and all heaven's varied moods,
by which You nourish all that You have made,
we praise You, O Lord.

For our Sister Water,
so useful, lowly, precious, and pure
we praise You, O Lord.

For our Brother Fire,
who brightens up our darkest nights,
(Beautiful is he and eager, invincible and keen)
we praise You, O Lord.

For our Mother earth,
who sustains and feeds us, producing fair fruits,
  many-colored flowers, and herbs
we praise You, O Lord.

For those who forgive one another for love of You
and who patiently bear sickness and other trials
(happy are they who peacefully endure;
You will crown them, O Most High)
we praise You, O Lord.

For our Sister Death,
the inescapable fact of life
(Woe to those who die in mortal sin!
Happy those she finds doing Your will!

From the Second Death they stand immune)
we praise You, O Lord.

All creatures, praise and glorify my Lord
and give Him thanks
and serve Him in great humility.

Saint Francis of Assisi

Prayer for Peace

Most holy God, the source of all good desires, all right
judgments, and all just works: Give to us, Your servants,
that peace which the world cannot give, so that our minds
may be fixed on the doing of Your will, and that we, being
delivered from the fear of all enemies, may live in peace and
quietness; through the mercies of Christ Jesus, our Savior.
AMEN.

Prayer of Thanksgiving

Almighty God, Father of all mercies,
we Your unworthy servants give You most humble and
    hearty thanks
for all Your goodness and loving-kindness
to us and to all whom You have made.
We bless You for our creation, preservation,
and all the blessings of this life;
but above all for Your immeasurable love
in the redemption of the world by our Lord Jesus Christ;
for the means of grace, and for the hope of glory.
And, we pray, give us such an awareness of Your mercies,
that our hearts may be sincerely thankful, and that we may
show forth Your praise
not only with our lips, but in our lives,
by giving up our selves to Your service,
and by walking before You
in holiness and righteousness all our days;

through Jesus Christ our Lord,
to whom, with You and the Holy Spirit,
be honor and glory throughout all ages. AMEN.

Te Deum

You are God: we praise You;
    You are the Lord: we acclaim You.
You are the eternal Father:
    All creation worships You.

To You all angels, all the powers of Heaven,
    Cherubim and Seraphim, sing in endless praise:
Holy, holy, holy Lord, God of power and might,
    Heaven and earth are full of Your glory.

The glorious company of apostles praise You.
    The noble fellowship of prophets praise You.
    The white-robed army of martyrs praise You.

Throughout the world the holy Church acclaims You:
    Father, of majesty unbounded,
Your true and only Son, worthy of all worship,
    and the Holy Spirit, advocate and guide.

You, Christ, are the King of glory,
    eternal Son of the Father.
When You became man to set us free,
    You did not shun the Virgin's womb.

You overcame the sting of death
    and opened the kingdom of Heaven to all believers.
You are seated at God's right hand in glory.
    We believe that You will come, and be our judge.

Come, then, Lord, help Your people,
    bought with the price of Your own blood,
and bring us with Your saints
    to glory everlasting.

Recommended Reading

Thomas Dubay:
> *The Fire Within* (the single most helpful book
> I have ever read about "advanced" prayer)

C. S. Lewis:
> *George Macdonald: An Anthology*
> *Letters to Malcolm: Chiefly on Prayer*
> *Reflections on the Psalms*

Thomas Merton:
> *The Ascent to Truth*
> *Seeds of Contemplation*

Ralph Martin:
> *Hungry for God*

Richard Foster:
> *Celebration of Discipline*
> *Freedom of Simplicity*

Elmer O'Brien, ed.:
> *Varieties of Mystical Experience*

W. H. Auden, ed.:
> *The Protestant Mystics*

R. A. Torrey:
> *How to Pray*

Merlin Carothers:
> *From Prison to Praise*
> *Power in Praise*

Hannah Hurnard:
> *Hinds' Feet on High Places*

Hannah Whitall Smith:
The Christian's Secret of a Happy Life

Brother Lawrence:
The Practice of the Presence of God

Lady Julian of Norwich:
Revelations of Divine Love

Saint John of the Cross:
The Ascent of Mount Carmel